Critical Incidents in Addictions Counseling

Edited by
Virginia A. Kelly
Gerald A. Juhnke

AMERICAN COUNSELING ASSOCIATION
5999 Stevenson Avenue
Alexandria, VA 22304
www.counseling.org

Critical Incidents in Addictions Counseling

10   9

American Counseling Association
5999 Stevenson Avenue
Alexandria, VA 22304

Director of Publications
Carolyn C. Baker

Production Manager
Bonny E. Gaston

Copy Editor
Elaine Dunn

Cover design by Scot Howard

Library of Congress Cataloging-in-Publication Data
Kelly, Virginia A.
   Critical incidents in addictions counseling/Virginia A. Kelly and Gerald A. Juhnke.
      p. cm.
   ISBN 1-55620-254-7 (alk. paper)
   ISBN 978-1-55620-254-4 (alk. paper)
   1.   Substance abuse—Patients—Counseling of—Case studies.   I.   Juhnke, Gerald A.   II.   Title.

   RC564.K465   2005
   362.29′186—dc22   2005001821

Table of Contents

Acknowledgments

We wish to acknowledge the contributors to *Critical Incidents in Addictions Counseling* for their efforts toward the completion of this publication, as well as their dedication to the field of addictions counseling. The contributors work in a variety of settings and capacities but share a common interest in assisting clients struggling with an addiction.

In addition, we wish to acknowledge Carolyn Baker, director of publications for the American Counseling Association. Her dedication to this project and her suggestions and feedback are greatly appreciated. Virginia Kelly would also like to acknowledge Kathleen Harder for her assistance and contributions to this book.

We would also like to acknowledge all of those individuals who work within the addictions field. This field represents a specialty within the counseling profession that focuses on issues that frequently co-occur for clients. These individuals have dedicated their professional lives to understanding this process in the hopes of assisting individuals in combating the issue of addiction.

Finally, it is important to note that a project like this could not be completed without the support and care of our family members. Thus, a very special "thank you" is expressed to Drew and Charlie Kelly, and Bryce, Brenna, and Debbie Juhnke.

Preface

*C*ritical Incidents in Addictions Counseling is a case-focused book that can be used by counselor educators, students, and clinicians to enhance their learning related to working with clients struggling with addictions. The format of the book is practical. In each chapter, a case involving addiction is described, followed by several questions posed by the incident author. The second portion of each chapter includes a response to the incident and the questions, generated by a professional within the addictions field.

The "incident" authors were asked to describe a case involving a specific aspect of addictions counseling (e.g., women's issues in addictions counseling, gambling addictions, Latinos and addictions counseling). This part of each chapter includes a description of the actual incident, along with an accounting of the treatment follow-up provided by the original counselor. Finally, these authors were asked to pose several questions regarding possible alternatives or supplemental strategies that might have enhanced treatment outcomes. The "incidents" were then sent to a professional within the addictions field who was asked to act as "responder" to that particular incident. These authors provided responses to the posed questions along with other observations and recommendations related to the presented case.

We worked to identify appropriate authors and edited both the incidents and responses. Individual authors were selected on the basis of their areas of expertise or practice within the field of addictions. Many of these individuals were identified through the International Association of Addictions and Offender Counselors division of the American Counseling Association (ACA). Authors were asked to address issues related to cultural implications, as well as ethics utilizing ACA's Code of Ethics and Standards for Practice (1995) and Multicultural Competencies (Arredondo et al., 1996; Roysircar, Arredondo, Fuertes, Ponterotto, & Toporek, 2003; Roysircar, Sandhu, & Bibbins, 2003; Sue, Arredondo, & McDavis, 1992).

We consider this book a beneficial resource that can be utilized as a supplemental text within an addictions course. Both beginning and advanced counselors can benefit from the integration of discussions related to specific cases involving a wide array of issues relating to addictions. It is expected that students can use these incidents to initiate discussion related to providing services to clients struggling with addiction along with other issues and challenges.

—Virginia A. Kelly and Gerald A. Juhnke

■References

American Counseling Association. (1995). *Code of ethics and standards of practice*. Alexandria, VA: Author.

Arredondo, P., Toporek, R., Brown, S. P., Jones, J., Locke, D., Sanchez, J., et al. (1996). Operationalization of the multicultural counseling competencies. *Journal of Multicultural Counseling and Development, 24,* 42–78.

Roysircar, G., Arredondo, P., Fuertes, J. N., Ponterotto, J. G., & Toporek, R. L. (2003). *Multicultural counseling competencies 2003.* Alexandria, VA: Association for Multicultural Counseling and Development.

Roysircar, G., Sandhu, D. S., & Bibbins, V. E., Sr. (2003). *Multicultural competencies: A guidebook of practices.* Alexandria, VA: Association for Multicultural Counseling and Development.

Sue, D. W., Arredondo, P., & McDavis, R. J. (1992). Multicultural competencies and standards: A call to the profession. *Journal of Counseling & Development, 70,* 477–486.

About the Editors

Virginia A. Kelly, PhD, is an associate professor in the Counselor Education Department at Fairfield University and can be reached at vkelly@mail.fairfield.edu.

Gerald A. Juhnke, EdD, is a professor and doctoral program director in the Department of Counseling, Educational Psychology, and Adult & Higher Education at the University of Texas at San Antonio and can be reached at gerald.juhnke@utsa.edu.

About the Authors

Michael Arthur, MS, NCC, LCPC, Bowdoin College

Wendy Charkow Bordeau, PhD, LPC, NCC, Georgian Court University

Ford Brooks, EdD, LPC, NCC, CAC, Shippensburg University

Kelly M. Burch-Ragan, PhD NCC, LMFT, LMHC, Western Kentucky University

Jane J. Carroll, PhD, LPC, NCC, MAC, CCAS, University of North Carolina at Charlotte

Catherine Y. Chang, PhD, LPC, NCC, Georgia State University

Stuart F. Chen-Hayes, PhD, NCC, Lehman College of the City University of New York

Kenneth M. Coll, PhD, LCPC, MAC, Boise State University

Marcheta P. Evans, PhD, LPC, NCC, University of Texas at San Antonio

James O. Fuller, PhD, LMHC, NCC, NCSC, Indiana Wesleyan University

Michael Tlanusta Garrett, PhD, Old Dominion University

Luke J. Gilleran, MA, NCC, private practice

Larry Golden, PhD, University of Texas at San Antonio

W. Bryce Hagedorn, PhD, LMHC, NCC, MAC, Florida International University

Joseph P. Jordan, MS, LPC, CCAS, CCS, MAC, partner, Family Solutions, PLLC

Gerald A. Juhnke, EdD, LPC, NCC, MAC, ACS, CCAS, University of Texas at San Antonio

Virginia A. Kelly, PhD, Fairfield University

Simone F. Lambert, PhD, LPC, NCC, Main Street Counseling, Creative Healing Institute

Pamela S. Lassiter, PhD, LPC, LMFT, CCAS, University of North Carolina at Charlotte

Todd F. Lewis, PhD, NCC , University of North Carolina at Greensboro

Robin Guill Liles, PhD, LPC, NCC, North Carolina Agricultural and Technical State University

David Lundberg, PhD, NCC, North Carolina Agricultural and Technical State University

Richard Madwid, MS, LPC, LADC, CCS, Fairfield University

Matthew Kent Mayberry, PhD, Augusta State University
Oliver J. Morgan, PhD, NCC, LMFT, ACS, DCA, University of Scranton
Cynthia J. Osborn, PhD, Kent State University
Nicole J. Pizzini, CADC, University of Iowa
Tracey E. Robert, PhD, LPC, NCCC, Fairfield University
Shawn L. Spurgeon, PhD, LPC, NCC, Western Kentucky University
Courtenay Trahan, MS, NCC, Fairfield Ludlowe High School
Albert A. Valadez, PhD, LPC, University of Texas at San Antonio
Laura J. Veach, PhD, LPC, CCAS, CCS, Wake Forest University
Kelly L. Wester, PhD, University of North Carolina at Greensboro

1
Counseling Impaired Professionals

Critical Incident

Ford Brooks

Background

Sam R., a 53-year-old White male, was referred by the state's medical society for an assessment of his alcohol and drug use. Sam had a history of alcohol use beginning in high school when he experienced his first blackout. A majority of his drinking at that time occurred on the weekends after sporting events. During the week, however, Sam was an exceptional student and graduated third in his class. He was admitted to an Ivy League school on an early decision because of his grade point average and extracurricular involvement with the debate team and student government.

As a child, Sam's home life, as he described it, was difficult at best. Both of his parents were raised in an alcoholic family, and during Sam's youth they both drank heavily. Sam's youngest sister was involved with drug use and eventually dropped out of high school and moved out on her own at the age of 16. Both of Sam's parents were lawyers, which typically meant late nights and heavy drinking after final court dispositions. In addition, Sam's house became the place where all his parents' friends would come and drink on the weekends. Professionals all, they would drink and occasionally smoke marijuana. On one occasion when he was 16, a female friend of his parents smoked pot with Sam in the basement, which became a regular occurrence.

Sam described a childhood of highs and lows. He said he was either "on top of the world" or "down in the dumps" depending on his environment. He found that athletics helped him increase his energy, which ultimately helped him pay attention in class. For Sam, school was easy, and at times he described it as "boring."

His anxiety, he believed, manifested in a skin condition, which he continues to battle with as an adult. His face, elbows, chest, and legs become red and itchy-flaky, particularly when stress is increased. He found this condition very disturbing during his adolescent years when he was dating. At that time he discovered how alcohol would make him feel "normal" and the incessant itching would cease. As a child he was called names such as "flaky boy" and "spotter," which brought about great embarrassment, sadness, and anger.

In college Sam drank only on the weekends, saving the weekday hours for study, as his plans were to enter medical school. He found as he drank in college how he was able to consume large amounts of alcohol and not feel intoxicated. He "won" many of the drinking contests in his fraternity and at the same time was voted most likely to succeed in life. He graduated with honors and was accepted into a prestigious medical school with hopes of studying emergency medicine.

In medical school Sam found the use of stimulants, along with the alcohol and periodic marijuana use, helpful in either keeping him awake to study or helping him to relax and sleep following demanding examinations. Halfway through medical school the Army sent Sam to Vietnam for one tour of duty as a medic. Throughout college and medical school he maintained an active status as a reservist and thus was enacted for active duty. In Vietnam he smoked opium and drank copious amounts of alcohol to survive the horrid conditions. Upon returning to the United States, he finished school and residency requirements, and settled into emergency medical work in a large metropolitan area.

Sam married after his return from Vietnam and has two children in college from that marriage. His wife divorced him after 10 years of marriage because of his continuous marijuana and alcohol use. Sam felt the divorce was due to his long hours at the hospital and his difficulty with communication. His two children lived with his wife until they entered college. Sam remarried 2 years later and is still married, albeit tenuously.

Incident

Sam was arrested for possession of an ounce of marijuana as well as an open container of beer while driving his car from work. Sam described that he typically, after a long shift at the hospital where he is employed, smokes a joint on the way home to his residence and drinks a beer to relax. One particular evening Sam was reaching for the lighter to ignite his marijuana cigarette and mistakenly bumped the steering wheel, thus making the car swerve. At that very moment a state trooper noticed the car swerve and followed Sam for 2 miles at which point he was pulled over for speeding and erratic driving. Upon approaching the driver's window, the trooper noticed the smell of marijuana and asked Sam to get out of the car, at which point the ounce of marijuana was discovered along with the open beer. Sam was taken to jail and charged with possession of marijuana, driving with an open container of alcohol, driving under the influence of alcohol/marijuana, and speeding. He was released after his wife posted bond. He contacted his lawyer and was instructed to turn himself in to the Medical Society before the licensing board got formally involved. He also has concerns that he will lose his employment as a medical supervisor.

The function of the Medical Society is to monitor impaired physicians, nurses, and health care workers. Sam wanted to obtain an alcohol and drug evaluation before his court date so he could tell the judge how remorseful and dedicated he was to investigating this incident. Sam has never had treatment for alcohol or drug addiction or any other psychiatric illness.

Upon entering the counselor's office, he said he would be tape recording the evaluation. He also stated that this was his second evaluation for his chemical use, that the last counselor "diagnosed me in 10 seconds as alcoholic and dependent on marijuana." Sam went on to state to this counselor, "My real problem is with this skin disorder and my moods. I don't have any difficulty with my using or drinking; in fact, it actually increases my ability to practice medicine more effectively."

The counselor allowed the taping to occur and initiated a number of questions to Sam regarding his most recent incident and chemical use. Sam appeared to be minimizing, compliant, and reluctant to describe frequencies and amounts. He challenged the academic degrees on the wall of the counselor's office and seemed curious about the training and background of the interviewer. Sam also was not willing to sign a release of information to his wife because "It is none of her business." Upon completion of the evaluation, the counselor recommended to Sam that he enter an inpatient program specifically designed to work with impaired professionals. At that point Sam became outraged and refused to pay the counselor for his services, claiming, "This is just one big rip-off; all you counselors are just the same." Realizing he needed a letter for court in 2 days, Sam's attitude changed, and he said to the counselor that he would think about it and agreed to pay for the evaluation. He also asked the counselor to write a letter to his attorney stating that he was evaluated but not to include the recommendation for inpatient treatment. Sam tentatively agreed to come to group counseling on an outpatient basis but would not enter an inpatient program unless he was told he had to by the court or by his employer.

Discussion

It was quite clear to the counselor how manipulative Sam was being and how Sam was in a great deal of denial surrounding his chemical use and the consequences associated with it. Sam appeared to focus on "other problems" and not his alcohol or drug use. When questioned by the counselor, Sam minimized and switched to other topics, making the evaluation diluted at best without data from Sam's wife.

Questions

1. Based on the information in Sam's background and current data presentation, what differential diagnosis might you have pursued in this evaluation? Based on this, what might be your initial treatment plan with him?
2. How might you have worked differently with Sam during the evaluation process regarding the recommendation? Would you have tailored the letter to Sam's liking?
3. How would you have responded to Sam's request to tape the evaluation session? Would you have allowed it? If so, why? If not, why not?

4. What interventions might you have used with Sam should you have worked with him in treatment?
5. Understanding that Sam is a physician, how might your work with him be different?
6. How would you have dealt with Sam's manipulation and narcissistic traits?

■Response

Cynthia J. Osborn

In several respects, Sam exemplifies a rather remarkable case in that, as a 53-year-old male physician with at least a 35-year history of substance use, he has managed to avert formal intervention or treatment until now. This suggests that he has apparently not experienced negative consequences of his substance use (other than perhaps his divorce), such as prior legal offenses, patient or staff formal complaints, malpractice claims, medical concerns, career/employment disruption, and/or financial difficulty. It could well be that Sam *has* experienced some or all of these and other negative effects directly related to his substance use; the assessment process has yet to capture them.

From Sam's case description, it is clear that he has been ambitious and tenacious, and has achieved a level of success in his chosen career. By his own report, certain things in his life have come easy for him, such as academic and athletic success, as well as maintaining employment in his chosen career. Perhaps management of his substance use up until this time has also come easy for him, typifying what has been referred to as being a "functional alcoholic" (Knapp, 1996) and living with a "well-maintained addiction" (DiClemente, 2003). Indeed, in Sam's mind, "winning" many of the drinking contests in his fraternity and being voted in college as the one most likely to succeed were not incompatible. It is probably reasonable to assume that Sam continues to view his current substance use and what appears to be his successful professional practice as two compatible practices. Hence, he may be asking, "What *is* all the fuss about? I messed up this once," and he might add, "So give me a break. Everyone makes mistakes. Now back off."

Although the pattern of his use in college appears to have been compartmentalized (i.e., using on specified days so as not to interfere with his studies), his subsequent use infiltrated what had earlier been "restricted" areas of his life. He appeared to regard this as a means of enhancing his academic and professional success (e.g., using stimulants to stay awake during medical school). Again, Sam may interpret this as further evidence that he can drink and smoke marijuana and still remain a successful emergency physician and medical supervisor. However, I am curious as to what has been taking place of late that has aggravated his earlier compartmentalized addiction and also thwarted his attempts to continue to use without his career being threatened. That is, how would Sam explain his substance use "getting out of hand" to the point that it was recently noticed by a police officer? What is taking place in his life right now that is making it more difficult for him to "keep the lid on" his substance use?

Differential Diagnosis

I believe that there is limited information presented in the case to confidently assign an indisputable diagnosis at this point. Other than the incident for which Sam was recently arrested, it is not clear yet how much and how often he has been using alcohol and marijuana in recent months. It is still unknown exactly how his substance use has negatively impacted his functioning (e.g., prior legal offenses, difficulty fulfilling work and family roles), and tolerance and withdrawal have yet to be assessed.

Sam's use of substances after a long shift at the hospital to relax is described as "typical," suggesting that such use has become a welcome part of his life that he incorporated into his lifestyle and routine. In his mind perhaps, using was essential for what he might characterize as a very stressful and demanding line of work. Given his regular use of substances in dangerous settings (i.e., while operating a motor vehicle), his regard for such use as necessary (i.e., to relax), and his long history of what seems to be regular use (beginning at approximately 16 years of age), I would probably assign both an alcohol dependence diagnosis and a cannabis dependence diagnosis. I would explain to Sam that such diagnoses are preliminary and could certainly change with additional information.

Treatment Recommendation

I would commend Sam for being proactive in obtaining an alcohol and drug evaluation prior to his court date. I would also commend him for following his attorney's advice and contacting the Medical Society before the licensing board became involved. This demonstrates initiative on his part consistent with his career achievements.

I would explain to Sam that, as an ethical practitioner concerned for his well-being and that of his patients and family, I am recommending his entrance in a specialized program designed specifically for physicians with substance use problems. Such a program, I would explain, is the best treatment selection at this time, one that would be tailored just for him and one that he deserves. I would appeal to Sam that, as an emergency physician and a medical supervisor, he should be able to appreciate my ethical obligation (and genuine desire) to provide services commensurate with the diagnosis. I would explain that a substance dependence diagnosis for someone in the helping profession warrants inpatient treatment in a specialized program and that this would be included in my letter to the court. I would further explain that his cooperation with such a recommendation might actually be in his favor with the court and would more than likely lessen the likelihood of other incidents (e.g., legal offenses, patient complaints, and familial concern and disruption) occurring. Pending entrance into such a program (based on bed availability and Sam arranging for coverage at the hospital), I would recommend his participation in intensive outpatient treatment, both individual and group.

Audio-Recording Request

I would have inquired about Sam's rationale for audiotaping our first session and would have requested (required?) the drafting and mutual signage of an audiotaping consent form, complete with how the recording would be used and who would gain possession and have access to it. I would explain to Sam that such a formalized, written agreement is consistent with how I work with clients and that, as a professional, I would expect nothing less from a client's request to audiotape our session. I would assume that my expectation of a written agreement is consistent with his own professional and ethical medical practice, particularly as a medical supervisor, thus validating and making use of Sam's own expertise. I would advise Sam, however, that the court might subpoena such a recording if its existence became known, which might deter him from proceeding with the recording.

Interventions Used

I would spend a considerable amount of time in this early phase learning as much as I could about Sam, including his substance use history. I would regard him as someone in the precontemplation stage of change (Prochaska, DiClemente, & Norcross, 1992), that is, someone unaware (or underaware) of the problem for which he has been referred to counseling, someone who is not yet able to assume responsibility or ownership for change. Indeed, Sam is one who does not believe that any change on his part is necessary. Rather, if change is to occur, it must be external change, that is, change in the Medical Society, the legal system, his wife, his skin disorder, or the counselor's expectations. Such presentation should not be surprising and, to some degree, is expected, given Sam's relatively long history of substance use without negative consequences or intervention.

I would not expect Sam to be any more ready to change than he is at this early phase. This would entail accepting his concerns or explanations as valid (e.g., "In your mind, your skin disorder is a priority, more so than your substance use. In fact, you can actually see that your drinking and smoking *enhance* your clinical practice") and attempting to understand Sam's life from his perspective ("You've been cruising along for the past 35 years with 'no problems,' and then all of a sudden someone is trying to make a big deal about your drinking and smoking and I surface with this grand idea of inpatient treatment"). This would be one way of joining with Sam, establishing preliminary rapport and a working alliance, essential for the counselor working with someone in the precontemplation stage of change (Miller, 1999), particularly one DiClemente (2003) might characterize as "rebellious" and not to be argued with.

I would understand Sam's lack of regard for representatives of the legal system, given his "insider's view" as a child of two lawyers who routinely engaged in "heavy drinking" with colleagues after finalizing court cases. I would therefore not attempt to convince Sam of his need to comply with the court, but would matter-of-factly present the challenge he is faced with and the choices that are his to make.

Working With Physician as Client

I would expect that Sam would be upset about needing to participate in an evaluation of his substance use. Given that male physicians with substance use concerns often enter treatment for work-related concerns (McGovern, Angres, Shaw, & Rawal, 2003), I would not find it unusual that Sam was not "owning up to" his problematic substance use in this first session. Indeed, as a medical supervisor in an emergency setting in a large metropolitan area, Sam's anger with what he might consider to be "taking orders," that is, complying with my "prescription" of inpatient drug and alcohol treatment, an invasive and disruptive intervention, would be understandable. This would be especially true given his skepticism about my credentials and qualifications. Sam is accustomed to being the authority figure, the one "giving orders." Listening to and cooperating with recommendations from a nonmedical "underling" is understandably difficult for Sam to swallow.

I would conduct a thorough assessment, requesting a baseline urine screen, having him complete an inventory such as the Addiction Severity Index, and obtaining permission to have contact with his wife and possibly a coworker. I would then present the information obtained from these sources in an objective and nonjudgmental manner (similar to the X-rays and lab results he might be accustomed to sharing with his own patients). I would share my professional opinion that this information would be important for him to consider in making decisions about his care. I would hope that my attempt at raising his awareness about his current circumstance would be viewed by Sam as professional collaboration, rather than delivering authoritative prescriptions and dictatorial pronouncements. I would convey to him that he is the expert on his own experiences and that his views and opinions matter in this decision-making process.

Personality Traits

What has been characterized as Sam's current state of "denial" and his "narcissistic" and "manipulative" tendencies may be quite understandable at this early phase of intervention. My preference, however, would be not to use these convenient and nomothetic or broad-brushed categorical explanations for Sam's behavior, which can have the effect of overlooking idiosyncratic information necessary in developing empathy for Sam. In addition, such labeling exonerates the clinician from having any responsibility in the process of change. That is, assigning problematic tendencies to Sam can be used as a convenient excuse for any lack of progress. The counselor, however, is charged with the responsibility of working collaboratively with Sam to assist in transitioning toward a readiness for change. Such movement is not something for the counselor to expect Sam to do on his own; if this were possible, Sam would not need to be in counseling.

To effectively work with Sam, the counselor needs to be able to appreciate the very early stage of change Sam is in. From Sam's perspective, he has come up against a reality incongruent with his familiar and (in his mind) problem-free lifestyle. Additional time is needed for him to be able to adjust to this new reality, and perhaps identity of himself. The counselor will do well to work cooperatively with Sam, which entails having a greater appreciation for Sam's perspective, his experience, and interacting with him as the professional that he is.

■References

DiClemente, C. C. (2003). *Addiction and change: How addictions develop and addicted people recover*. New York: Guilford Press.

Knapp, C. (1996). *Drinking: A love story*. New York: Dial Press.

McGovern, M. P., Angres, D. H., Shaw, M., & Rawal, P. (2003). Gender of physicians with substance use disorders: Clinical characteristics, treatment utilization, and post-treatment functioning. *Substance Use & Misuse, 38,* 993–1001.

Miller, W. R. (Ed.). (1999). *Enhancing motivation for change in substance abuse treatment: Treatment Improvement Protocol Series 35* (DHHS Publication No. SMA 99-3354). Rockville, MD: U.S. Department of Health and Human Services.

Prochaska, J. O., DiClemente, C. C., & Norcross, J. C. (1992). In search of how people change: Applications to addictive behaviors. *American Psychologist, 47,* 1102–1114.

2
Counseling Addicted Families

■Critical Incident

Simone F. Lambert

Background

John is an 18-year-old Caucasian male who at the time of services resided with his father. He was referred to me for counseling services through his father's Employee Assistance Program. After completion of his authorized sessions, it was clear that John was in need of additional treatment, and he chose to continue our work together in the private practice setting. His initial presenting problem was excessive drinking, which led to numerous difficulties. At the time, the most pressing concern was a lack of direction as the client had just failed all of his classes in his first semester of college. After completing the Brief Michigan Alcohol Screening Test (MAST), the Alcohol Abstinence Self-Efficacy Scale, and the Drinking Related Internal–External Locus of Control Scale and examining the *Diagnostic and Statistical Manual of Mental Disorders* (4th ed., Text Revision [*DSM-IV-TR*]; American Psychiatric Association, 2000) criteria, it was clear that John did meet the diagnosis for substance abuse.

While using a cognitive-behavioral approach with John, we discussed making effective choices based on the pros and cons of anticipated outcomes. In the past, John's decision-making process was based on satisfying his immediate desires rather than worrying about consequences. In fact, throughout high school he had been using alcohol, marijuana, and occasionally other substances with little or no consequences that he could identify. He had become a master of deception to cover his use and to cover the negative impact that his drinking and lying was having on him. There were petty alcohol citations in the past, but these were of no real consequence because he was a minor at that time.

John's parents divorced when he was a sophomore in high school. He denied that this was the incident that led him to begin his substance use. However, his home life with his mother was tumultuous to say the least. He maintained a positive relationship with his father but was only able to spend every other weekend at his father's home, because of a custody agreement that was set until John reached the age of 18. His older brother, Eric, also had difficulties with his mother yet seemed to be able to handle his anger better. Eric experimented with alcohol and had some similar incidents as well. However, Eric seemed to overcome these challenges on his own and conversely became quite successful in his academic career. The only reported family history of substance abuse was the paternal grandmother, who reportedly "drank a lot."

Incident

There were three major incidents (or wake-up calls) during this case. The first was when the client obtained a DWI after going to a party. He began drinking at the party because his "girlfriend" was talking to other guys. We had discussed how in the past the client has had feelings of awkwardness in social situations (especially when talking with a girl) and feelings of empowerment through drinking. His thoughts prior to choosing to drink were that he would not be held responsible for his actions because he could always blame the alcohol if he did not get the social results he wanted. Even after discussing the possibility of drinking and possible consequences prior to the party, John chose to have a beer. One became two, two became three, and so on. He finally left the party upset, defeated, and intoxicated. The result of the ensuing DWI that night was limitations on his driver's license, court and lawyer fees, a penalty fine, and alcohol education classes administered by the county.

At this point in treatment, his father, John, and I examined whether more intensive services were needed. The client had previously denied diagnosis of substance abuse, but he was starting to see that his alcohol use was a real issue. John's father was concerned about John's safety. All agreed to biweekly individual counseling sessions and AA meetings at a minimum of five times a week to decrease the likelihood of inpatient counseling or a more structured outpatient counseling program.

The next major incident came when John had regained a little of his father's faith. His father let him stay at his home unsupervised for a week rather than go to his mother's house, which John did not want to do. The initial story given to the counselor and to his father by the client was inaccurate; apparently, John in fact had invited a few friends over for a party the first weekend of his father's absence. One of the very inebriated attendees proceeded to wreck his car on John's lawn and sustained significant injuries. John denied drinking at this event and reported that he was not interested in drinking after seeing the gruesome wounds of his party acquaintance. His father again returned to the next session to ensure that I had heard the full story, which up until that time I had not.

The last major incident was a month later when John again chose to drive home after drinking a beer at his friend's house. This time he flipped his car and escaped with a mere injury to his arm. This accident could have resulted in death. While John was given a DUI citation, he reported feeling lucky and grateful to have another chance. Again his father came to session. Actually, his intention was just to drop off John since his license had been suspended at that

Critical Incidents in Addictions Counseling

point. His father further reiterated his support and love of his son but not of John's past actions. At this point, John had to maintain sobriety and academic performance to continue receiving financial backing from his father. John also now faced the adult consequences of not being able to drive for a year, a record that may impede his procurement of a well-paying job, and possible jail time. The critical incident occurred at this point. John realized that he had to change his behaviors or he could lose everything.

Cognitive-Behavioral Approach

John did not follow the recommendations of biweekly counseling in conjunction to AA meetings. He came only for weekly counseling sessions and reportedly could not find an AA group that he felt comfortable attending. During the counseling sessions we focused on how his thoughts and feelings contributed to his past actions. This empowered the client to take a different path by changing those past patterns.

John was assigned journaling, and he reported limited benefit to this exercise at first. He seemed to be numb or disconnected to his inner self. After the critical incident, he began to do some soul-searching and found the journaling to be an effective medium for examining his motives for past actions. He realized that he did not want to dig himself into a hole deeper than he had already.

Throughout counseling sessions we discussed how John's past behavior indicated that he cannot drink and get the long-term results he desires. We also examined the pattern of self-sabotage. Before each major incident, he had made significant progress in other areas of his life (i.e., school, work, accountability, relationship with his father). In the end, John decided that in order to prove to himself he must be more independent and take all responsibility for his actions.

Discussion

John was a bright young adult who throughout his 4 months of counseling was able to maintain two jobs and succeed in classes at a community college. He became intrinsically motivated for treatment, upon discovering that the only person who really was being hurt by his actions was himself. John maintained sobriety following the critical incident and continued making progress on discovering himself and defining his life goals.

Questions

1. While his father attended sessions as needed to provide support and encouragement and to establish consequences, John's mother did not attend sessions. Given the impact that this relationship had on the client and that it was an identified trigger for him, would it have been beneficial to include her in the treatment? If so, should his father be present as well during those sessions?
2. Because the client showed poor decision making with escalating consequences, was there another intervention that could have been implemented

after the DWI and before the DUI? Keep in mind that inpatient facilities were consulted and the client did not meet the criteria for admission.

3. What developmental issues were factors in this case? How did John's transition from childhood to adulthood play a role in his conceptualization of the situation?
4. Was John's father a necessary support system or an enabler?
5. Should the counselor have enforced the recommendation of biweekly counseling session and attendance of AA meetings as agreed on? If so, how?

■Response

Wendy Charkow Bordeau

The counselor, in her description of case dynamics, conceptualization, intervention, and follow-up questions, displays impressive assessment and treatment skills, as well as an obvious sense of professionalism and ultimate concern for the well-being of the adolescent client and his family. This case sounds difficult for several reasons. First, the client obviously has a long history of manipulation that he brought into the counseling relationship. As he presented with an abundant supply of denial and rationalization defenses, this counselor had to tread the thin line between establishing rapport and engaging the client in the therapeutic process while also holding the client accountable for his statements and behaviors.

Second, as John is an 18-year-old college student living in his father's home, he is in the challenging developmental stage of the transitional adolescent– adult. Though he is legally no longer a minor, he still has to abide by parental rules while establishing himself as an autonomous individual. It sounds as though, at least at the onset of counseling, that John did not perceive much motivation for alleviation of symptoms or lifestyle changes, largely as he did not have to rely on himself for the fulfillment of his practical and financial needs. Similarly, he no longer has the supportive community of concerned adults in a high school environment who can watch out for him and provide information and assistance to him and his family. The counselor posed the question of how John's developmental issues played a role in his conceptualization of his situation. In addition to what has previously been said, I also believe that John is just learning to see the long-term consequences of his behavior and, unfortunately, these "critical incidents" are often necessary to spur adolescents to see the link between their current behavior and long-term well-being, as well as to develop the ability to defer gratification. It certainly is difficult for counselors and parents to stand back and watch adolescents make what look like preventable mistakes; however, it has long been established that experiential learning is often the only method for developmental progress and behavior changes in situations in which the adolescent has built such strong defenses and compensations for his actions.

Concomitantly, it was obvious that John's father was experiencing difficulty negotiating his role of father to a burgeoning adult with concurrent dependency/

autonomy needs and probably gave inconsistent messages about what he expected from both his son and the counselor. Confidentiality and client loyalty issues easily could have come into play had John's father demanded information from the counselor regarding his son or further expressed his own needs and anxieties. I also suspect that John's father suffered a great deal of guilt surrounding his divorce, loss of custody, and the seemingly negative consequences to his children. I imagine that he, as would most any parent in this situation, has continually struggled to balance child discipline and structure with his desire for a pleasant and loving relationship with his sons. The counselor pondered whether John's father served as a necessary support system or an enabler to his son. My response is, similar to most parents of substance abusers, probably a little bit of both. It is obvious that John's father is deeply concerned for his son and should be supported in his difficult parenting task. Some enabling behavior is evident in the situation in which he allowed John to stay unsupervised in the house for a week because he did not want to go to his mother's house following his first DWI. Although "hindsight is 20/20," this decision most likely led to a situation in which most adolescents addicted to alcohol would fall prey to the impulse to drink and invite friends over to an empty house. Therefore, I think John's father may benefit from attendance at Al-Anon or another parent support meeting in which he could meet with other parents also struggling with adult children with alcohol problems. John's father might also benefit from further exploring his own thoughts and feelings about his own mother's alcohol use and how this affects John's substance abuse and the current parent–child relationships.

Finally, John appears to be a challenging client as his symptoms fall in the "borderline" range in which they are certainly dangerous enough to incur a serious risk to the welfare of himself and others but not considered severe to the point that an inpatient placement could always be justified to third-party payment sources. Additionally, he would most likely not have fulfilled criteria for involuntary placement in the likely event that he would refuse to enter inpatient treatment on his own. Therefore, he needed to be maintained in a minimally restrictive environment with opportunities for behavioral change though the counselor and father had no real way to constantly monitor his actions and guarantee his safety. Much easier said than done! Simply stated, any counselor in this case would and should feel some degree of confusion in determining the best methods for proceeding. Case consultation and supervision are often helpful and necessary in this type of counseling scenario.

I agree that the cognitive-behavioral approach used in this case was appropriate as John presented with several faulty cognitions that most likely led to many of his behavioral problems. For example, he believed that "I am not to be held responsible for my actions when I am under the influence of alcohol." If this was truly the case, then who would not opt to engage in substance use to deal with every difficult life situation? Another initial faulty belief that contributed to his deterioration was the idea that his drinking was disconnected from his obvious academic and social struggles. It appears that the cognitive-behavioral methods used by this counselor allowed the client to grapple with and revise these distorted notions over the course of counseling. Motivational interviewing, in which the client would be asked to explore both the advantages and disadvantages to his substance use, sounds as though it was implemented with positive results. I also commend the counselor's astute observation of the self-sabotage dynamic present in this client's life. I agree that until John acknowledged, explored, and revised his fear of success that he would unlikely make sustainable progress in counseling.

The counselor also questions whether inclusion of the mother in the counseling process could have led to quicker and more in-depth therapeutic gains. I am certainly a proponent of involving significant others in the counseling process, especially when their involvement (or lack thereof) appears to contribute significantly to the presenting problem. In this case, it is obvious that issues related to the divorce and subsequent custody arrangements need to be further explored and resolved for the client to fully accept his family situation and feel more confident in his abilities to maintain adult relationships without resorting to regressive behaviors and substance use. However, I do not believe there is enough information presented to make a clear determination about how to best involve the mother.

Some questions I would like to address further if given the opportunity include the following: What specific dynamics existed in the "tumultuous" home life when John lived in custody of his mother? For example, was there any history of abuse or neglect? My hunch is that John's mother vacillated between strict discipline tactics and permissive parenting and possibly displaced her anger at her husband toward her two almost grown sons. Of course I would want to investigate this hunch more before going further. Also, what type of relationship exists currently between John and his mother? It appears to be very distant, but perhaps there is also a degree of symbiosis in which he "plays" one parent against the other? Without the mother's input, it would be difficult to answer these questions. Also, what was the temporal relationship between the parental divorce and the development of substance-abusing behaviors? I would probably proceed by indicating to the client and his father that family issues most likely contributed to John's current situation and would best be resolved only through the involvement of all key players, including John's mother and brother. I am especially interested in hearing how the brother overcame his tendencies toward substance abuse and succeeded in his academic career while also experiencing similar levels of family problems. I would like to see how Eric could support John and serve as a role model while also being cognizant to not make too many comparisons and expect that John follow too closely in his brother's footsteps.

How to best include these family members in counseling would have to be decided after discussing this further with them, assessing their reactions to this suggestion, and cocreating a plan that would be palatable for all involved parties. I would also imagine that John and his mother would benefit from at least one or two sessions in which they could explore the issues in their relationship and how they affect John's behavior without the presence of the father. Perhaps after mother and son worked out some relational "kinks," the three of them could meet to discuss together how coparenting will proceed. This is especially important, as John has shown that he is not ready to be in the house by himself for extended periods of time and there are times when John's father needs to leave him unsupervised. Additionally, if John relapses and the decision to use a "tough love" approach is made, the parents will need to be in communication and accord with one another regarding how to handle the situation.

The counselor also inquired whether it would have been possible to implement an intervention that could have possibly prevented the DUI and whether she should have more strongly enforced the recommendation of biweekly counseling sessions and attendance of AA meetings as agreed on in the beginning. I see these questions as related because, though I do not think any outpatient counselor has the ability to always protect clients from themselves (and sometimes we need to learn from our mistakes), I wonder if stronger enforcement of the agreed-on treatment conditions may have impacted the client in such a way that he would not have had the opportunity to incur another DUI. Of course, the counselor's "hands are tied" as she cannot force him to go to these meetings and the responsibility for his life is ultimately his own.

However, I do believe that John may have taken away the message from counseling that, as perhaps similar to his home environment, "If I say the right things, I don't need to follow the rules they are putting out before me." It is my experience that clients commonly indicate that they cannot find a 12-step meeting in which they feel comfortable. I try to use this opportunity to discuss the idea that it is important to ultimately find a long-term group that feels "right"; however, this can take time and will happen only if the client continues to try different meetings. I also suggest that the client look for speaker meetings to attend when trying a new group so he can start as more of an observer and then participate more fully as his comfort level rises. Of course, I think most often clients indicate they cannot find a meeting when they have not really tried or are not invested. Therefore, I would want to ask John directly what was keeping him from looking for other meetings and continually challenge anything that sounds like an excuse. This is important because individual counseling is not likely sufficient to work through his denial and minimization, and I believe he needs to witness the experience of others in similar situations, who are "on to" the defense dynamics, to fully realize the severity of his behavior. Perhaps a contingency contract signed at the onset of counseling or when the situation worsened, with consequences of losing the father's financial and practical support, could have been used as a stronger basis for treatment compliance.

In conclusion, I am grateful to the counselor for sharing this case. Unfortunately, the dynamics present in this client's life are very common and need to be addressed by most counselors working in the field of addictions and adolescent counseling. I believe this counselor did an outstanding job, especially in light of the many inherent complexities. One of the most important lessons I think we can learn from this counseling scenario and the many similar others is to be aware of how hard it is to balance concern for client welfare and autonomy, and constantly explore potential countertransference issues as we work to deftly combine therapeutic respect, rapport, exploration, and limit-setting.

■Reference

Americna Psychiatric Association. (2000). *Diagnostic and statistical manual of mental disorders* (4th ed., Text Revision). Washington, DC: Author.

Critical Incidents in Addictions Counseling

3
Women's Issues in Addictions

■Critical Incident

Tracey E. Robert

Background

I have been a career counselor for 20 years and have had my private practice focusing on adults and career transition for 15 of those years. My services include individual and group counseling, career assessment, coaching, and consulting. I also provide Employee Assistance Program (EAP) services to area corporations.

One year ago, Evelyn, a 51-year-old, married, Caucasian female, was referred to me by her employer's EAP program for career development services. Evelyn was a full-time employee of Generad, a medical marketing firm, for 10 years. She had started as an office manager and was promoted 2 years ago to the position of manager of meeting planning. Her responsibilities included planning all medical education meetings for clients and supervising two support staff. As her referral stated, Evelyn had expressed dissatisfaction with her work and was feeling stress regarding her career options and future in the current job. In Evelyn's words, "I just don't know what to do. I know I don't want to continue doing what I'm doing."

During intake, Evelyn provided a work and educational history. She was married with two adult male children, ages 23 and 25. Both sons had attended college and graduated and currently live in other states and are fully employed in the career fields of their choice. Evelyn described her sons as smart, caring, and very capable adults. Evelyn described her husband, a full-time international marketing executive for a Fortune 500 company, as talented, energetic, and supportive. They had been married for 33 years.

Evelyn's educational background included a bachelor's degree in English from a woman's college and a 6-month certificate in administration from a business school. She had met her husband in college and planned to work until she had children. She accepted a job after college while she planned her wedding and worked full time as an assistant to the vice president of marketing for an advertising agency. Upon the birth of her first child, she resigned and became a full-time mother and homemaker. Evelyn was active in her community, serving on committees for the Young Women's Club in her town and then actively attending PTA functions and helping with the school newsletter. With the birth of her second son, she continued to be involved with her children's activities and joined a book club with the local public library.

As her children entered high school, Evelyn and her husband decided she needed to go back to work to help defray the costs of college education. She reentered the workforce through the help of a contact of her husband's who referred her to her current employer. She started in the position of office manager for a start-up firm offering medical education services to hospitals and doctors. Evelyn felt very excited and grateful that someone hired her, and she enjoyed being the "right-hand person" of the owner of the firm. She described liking the fact that she got in on the ground floor and helped establish the meeting planning department. After 8 years of working in that capacity, she was promoted to manager of the department.

Incident

Many employees find that when they reach the maintenance stage of a job, they lose interest and motivation and do not know where to turn for help. They often seek career counseling, thinking that they need to change fields and do something entirely new to feel energized. Upon entering counseling a year ago, Evelyn expressed these feelings, and we started on a journey of discovery, including career assessment and career exploration activities. Evelyn's knowledge of the work world was fairly narrow, and this year of focused exploration was helpful in widening her view of career options and possibilities. However, during the last session when Evelyn was starting to put together her plan of action, she broke down in tears. She revealed that she did not see how she could follow through and make a change at this point in her life. She was too old to be of service, her company was being sold, and the original owner, whom she was very dedicated to, was retiring. The new company was already coming in with changes, and she felt pressure to perform at a level she was unprepared for and possibly not interested in. Her husband was too busy with his career to offer support. He had been through four changes of management over the years and he just shrugged it off. Her sons were very involved in the development of their careers and new lives and told her that things would work out. Evelyn also revealed that she had been drinking three to four glasses of wine a night for the past year. She said she needed to relax when she came home and prepared dinner and waited for her husband to come home. By the time he arrived, she had already had two to three glasses. She said this helped her keep the conversation going over dinner and helped her feel calm about her hectic day. She said she did not see this as affecting her performance at work and she never drank before 6 p.m., so she did not see it as a problem. She did report that she could not remember doing certain things at home like cleaning up after dinner or finishing chores she had started. In addition, she remarked that she seemed to be bumping into things a lot since she kept finding black and blue marks on her legs and did not know where they came from.

Critical Incidents in Addictions Counseling

Discussion

During this disclosure, I asked Evelyn if she had discussed this information with her doctor or EAP counselor. She said she had never talked about it before. I asked her if she understood the effects of alcohol use in women and how this might be affecting her physically as well as emotionally, psychologically, and spiritually. She said her husband drank every night and he was okay. We then discussed the physiological differences between men and women with regard to alcohol addiction. Evelyn was unaware of the fact that women have less body water than men and this affects alcohol absorption rates and dependence issues.

According to recent research by the National Institute on Alcohol Abuse and Alcoholism (U.S. Department of Health and Human Services, 1995), the amount of alcohol that Evelyn had been drinking daily was considered abuse. I shared this information with her and explained some of the possible physical effects. I decided to do a substance abuse assessment using the questions from the Substance Abuse Subtle Screening Inventory (SASSI). Evelyn agreed to answer the questions as truthfully as possible. My concerns were that Evelyn was hiding her drinking and did not understand the possible debilitating effects on her relationships, work, and physical well-being. I emphasized that this was a serious issue and that working with her career and personal issues at the same time would be helpful. I referred her to Web sites for information about women and drinking and also gave her the locations and times of local AA meetings. She was reluctant to attend any near her home but felt she might go to a meeting near her work since it was in another county. I also referred her to her EAP office for further information and to ask for a referral to an addiction specialist. We contracted to meet one more time to follow up on her referrals.

Questions

1. Given the nature of alcohol addiction in women, what additional interventions might you have used with Evelyn?
2. Given the life stage that Evelyn was in, what other issues might be contributing to her addiction?
3. Are there any confidentiality issues to be addressed with this case?
4. How would you resolve the career counseling process?

■Response

Jane J. Carroll

The systematic and wide-ranging initial interview with the client provided much helpful information about the client's perspective on her circumstances, particularly her analysis of the state of affairs of her professional career and her drinking behavior. Counselors working in EAPs see the extent to which difficulties in the workplace can influence employees' use of alcohol. According to

Ansbacher and Ansbacher (1956), Adler wrote that individuals need to feel satisfaction in their work. Furthermore, Adler stated that people develop a private logic, a philosophy about themselves, their lives, and their relationships with others that guides their behavior. In this client's case, it is possible that the client's belief that she cannot meet performance standards or adjust to the current workplace changes, as well as being unprepared to compete in the workplace, has contributed to her use of alcohol. The client provided less information about her perceptions of the character and quality of her relationships with her husband and sons. Knowing that abusing substances likely affects all areas of an individual's life, I can develop answers to the questions posed by the referral source, a career counselor. Without ignoring the pervasiveness of the effects of alcohol abuse, therefore, I primarily will address with the referring counselor the impact drinking may have on the client's work situation and career outlook.

The first question the referring source asked was: *Given the nature of alcohol addiction in women, what additional interventions might you have used with Evelyn?*

"Addiction" is a lay term denoting substance dependence. It often is used, however, in clinical conversations. Given the data available, I agree with the referring counselor's assessment that the client, Evelyn, is abusing alcohol, rather than being dependent on it. I see no evidence of alcohol dependence as it is described in the *Diagnostic and Statistical Manual of Mental Disorders* (4th ed., Text Revision [*DSM-IV-TR*]; American Psychiatric Association, 2000).

Evelyn's substance-abusing behavior, however, calls for further exploration and continuing attention. Evelyn has never been diagnosed as substance dependent; however, she exhibits ongoing substance use despite recurrent interpersonal problems that are caused or exacerbated by the effects of the alcohol (American Psychiatric Association, 2000). To support this diagnosis, I call attention to Evelyn's

- drinking habitually in amount, timing, and frequency, and doing so for the past year
- experiencing amnesia ("blackouts") related to drinking
- concealing the extent to which she uses alcohol
- using alcohol to alter her mood
- using alcohol as an effort to increase her sociability with her husband
- displaying inexplicable bruises on her legs
- comparing her drinking with that of her husband as a standard for acceptability

I commend the referring counselor, a career counselor, for taking steps to educate Evelyn about alcohol use and abuse and the resources available to her. Moreover, I think it was a sound decision for the referring counselor to ask the EAP office at Evelyn's workplace for a referral for Evelyn to an addictions specialist. Evelyn's alcohol use is biologically, psychologically, sociologically, and perhaps spiritually linked. For that reason, the referring counselor also could have helped Evelyn in ways that are described below.

Critical Incidents in Addictions Counseling

Other interventions the referring counselor could have provided for Evelyn include the following:

1. Assess Evelyn's motivation to seek help from an addictions specialist or to otherwise take steps toward changing her drinking behavior. The subject of motivation is raised because Evelyn stated she does not think she has a problem, even in the light of meeting professionally recognized criteria for substance abuse. The transtheoretical model developed by Prochaska and DiClemente (1982) has been used extensively in assessing stages of change in addictions. Evelyn appears to be in the "reluctant precontemplation" stage because she does not think she has a problem (DiClemente, 1991, p. 192). In addition to the steps the counselor has already taken, strategies useful for this stage of change include developing trust with the client so that she feels at ease talking more fully about her drinking. In the meantime, respecting the client and being interested in what she hopes to achieve in all areas of life are important actions to take. When appropriate, help Evelyn make connections between substance abuse and her other problems.

2. Assess Evelyn's locus of control to determine the extent to which she feels in control over events in her life. Evidence that Evelyn may have an external locus of control include her being "grateful" that someone hired her, that she was "too old" to be of service, and that alcohol helped "keep the conversation going over dinner and helped her feel calm about her hectic day." Results from the Rotter (1966) scale may be of use to the career counselor in her current work with Evelyn and also for Evelyn's addictions counselor. This instrument is in the public domain and so is published online as well as in textbooks.

3. Measure Evelyn's level of morale and contentment by administering the Life Satisfaction Index—Form A (Neugarten, Havighurst, & Tobin, 1961). The results could provide data for the career counselor and the addictions counselor. This instrument also is in the public domain.

4. Discuss with Evelyn the socialization of women in the United States and the attitudes toward women's use of alcohol, in particular. It would not be prudent for several reasons, however, for the career counselor to address the shame and associated emotions Evelyn may be feeling. Because of the time-limited nature of their involvement and the often deep-seated reasons for shame, the referring counselor may defer discussing topics such as Evelyn's hiding her drinking and her reluctance to attend AA meetings near her home. Such behavior could be evidence of Evelyn feeling shame with roots in guilt about doing something "bad." Evelyn could be feeling shame and anxiety related to her perceptions of cultural and gender expectations of her as a woman.

The second question the referring source asked was: *Given the life stage that Evelyn was in, what other issues might be contributing to her addiction?*

Gilligan (1982) wrote that women learn from their mothers to be nurturing and to place a high priority on caring for others. Traditional models of development (e.g., Erikson, 1963) emphasize developing independence and autonomy. Gilligan wrote that, contrary to the men Erikson studied, women are searching for connectedness with others. Evelyn, at age 51, faces the need to make a choice in how she can arrange a feeling of connectedness in the workplace. She can continue on the challenging path of finding a new job or adapting to alterations in her current job. Evelyn reports she thinks she is unprepared for handling the newly assigned responsibilities at her current job. What is more, she would have to cope with the loss of familiar personnel and procedures at her workplace. Evelyn's dilemma fits both Erikson's description of middle-aged people struggling in the generativity versus stagnation stage and Gilligan's description of women's psychosocial need for relationships. Believing that being 51 limits her ability to be productive (generative) is shown in Evelyn's comment that she was "too old to be of service." The significance of relationships to her is found in at least three ways. First, Evelyn reacted emotionally while discussing the helplessness and sense of loss she felt about changes in her current work circumstances with which she is familiar and to which she has been committed. Second, she mentioned the lack of empathy expressed by her husband who was "too busy with his career." Finally, she articulated pride in her two adult sons who live at a distance from her.

Goals of counseling for Evelyn could include ways to strengthen relationships she currently has and to build new ones. The counselor can work toward those goals by focusing on improving Evelyn's concept of self-worth, providing a supportive and safe place in which she can explore feelings, gain insight, develop constructive coping skills, and learn how to adapt to stressors. The counselor also may want to explore Evelyn's recreational patterns. Less personal than relationships with people, but perhaps as consequential, would be helping Evelyn become involved with hobbies such as reading, crafts, card games, caring for pets, and collecting. Sports activities, whether as a participant or observer, also present opportunities for feeling connected or as a part of something bigger than oneself. Finally, Evelyn could be asked to talk about any religious and spiritual concerns she may have. To what extent is she involved in religious or spiritual activity, and is this an area of her life in which she would like to make some changes? Has her drinking affected her religious or spiritual beliefs or practices?

The third question the referring source asked was: *Are there any confidentiality issues to be addressed with this case?*

The referring counselor should be aware of ethical and legal responsibilities she has regarding confidentiality with this client. Clients have a right to privacy. Unless the counselor has reason to believe that Evelyn is a clear and present danger to herself or others or has knowledge of abuse or neglect of minor children or dependent adults, or unless a court orders release of information about Evelyn, the counselor cannot release information about Evelyn to anyone without the client's written permission. The release of information form Evelyn would sign must contain the following:

1. Name of client (Evelyn)
2. Name of person making disclosure (career counselor)
3. Purpose of disclosure
4. Who may receive information
5. Information to be released described exactly and as narrowly as possible
6. Statement that the client understands that she may revoke the consent at any time (except to the extent that action has been taken on it)
7. Statement that revocation may be oral or written
8. Date or when consent expires
9. Date consent form is signed
10. Signature of the client

Her employer referred Evelyn to the career counselor. EAPs are most effective when clients are assured of confidentiality. The employer is entitled only to the information that previously has been agreed to by Evelyn, the counselor, and the employer about Evelyn's contact with the career counselor. In addition, the counselor must make efforts in her private practice to ensure the confidentiality and safety of Evelyn's records. If, as a function of her counseling practice, the counselor employs or supervises other individuals who may see the client's records, the counselor must make efforts to maintain the client's confidentiality and privacy.

The federal guidelines for confidentiality (42 CFR) apply here if the counselor works with individuals receiving Medicaid. I have simplified the wording of 42 CFR as it may apply to this case. The rule prohibits the disclosure of a client's name and any other identifying information by individual practitioners who specialize in providing individualized *referral for substance abuse treatment and who are certified to receive Medicaid reimbursement* (Medicaid, 2004).

The last question asked by the referring source was: *How would you resolve the career counseling process?*

The referring counselor reported that she would meet with Evelyn one more time to follow up on the referrals. It is unclear at this time if Evelyn will take action on the proposals she has received from the counselor. Evelyn may not view the referring counselor's opinion that she abuses alcohol and might, therefore, benefit from addictions counseling and attending AA meetings as significant to her well-being. For Evelyn to be successful in changing employment or her outlook on her current position, however, it is essential that she analyze the causes and effects of her alcohol abuse. I suggest she undertake this task immediately with an addictions specialist, incorporating into their sessions the problems related to her work.

Real barriers to Evelyn's establishing clear career goals include her uncertainty about her role in the organization and her perceived lack of ability for the job. She may need help clarifying how she can keep up with new developments in the workplace and keep up with competition, while being aware that in the not-too-distant future she will be preparing to let go of her responsibilities and prepare for life outside the workplace. I suggest the career counselor use the data she has from the year of working with Evelyn to help her evaluate her strengths, assess her work options, and set new career goals. Further, the counselor could help Evelyn learn job-searching strategies and discuss with her the resources available to her in continuing education and training.

■References

American Psychiatric Association. (2000). *Diagnostic and statistical manual of mental disorders* (4th ed., Text Revision). Washington, DC: Author.

Ansbacher, H. L., & Ansbacher, R. R. (Eds.). (1956). *The individual psychology of Alfred Adler*. New York: Harper & Row.

DiClemente, C. C. (1991). Motivational interviewing and the stages of change. In W. R. Miller & S. Rollnick (Eds.), *Motivational interviewing: Preparing people to change addictive behavior* (pp. 191–202). New York: Guilford Press.

Erikson, E. H. (1963). *Childhood and society* (2nd ed.). New York: Norton.

Gilligan, C. (1982). *In a different voice*. Cambridge, MA: Harvard University Press.

Medicaid. (2004). *Medicaid alcohol and substance confidentiality restrictions*. Retrieved June 15, 2004, from https://www.emedny.org/ePACES/MedConfidentialityReg.aspx#General_1_2

Neugarten, B. L., Havighurst, R. J., & Tobin, S. S. (1961). The measurement of life satisfaction. *Journal of Gerontology, 16,* 134–143.

Prochaska, J. O., & DiClemente, C. C. (1982). Transtheoretical therapy: Toward a more integrative model of change. *Psychotherapy: Theory, Research, and Practice, 19,* 276–288.

Rotter, J. B. (1966). Generalized expectancies for internal versus external control of reinforcement. *Psychological Monographs, 80*(Whole No. 609).

U.S. Department of Health and Human Services. (1995). *The physician's guide to helping patients with alcohol problems* (NIH Publication No. 95-3769). Rockville, MD: Author. Retrieved May 20, 2004, from http://www.niaaa.nih.gov/publications/physicn.htm

4

Sexual Addiction as a Precursor to Chemical Addiction

■Critical Incident

W. Bryce Hagedorn

Background

Twenty-nine-year-old Enrique ("Rick") was admitted to our residential treatment facility for cocaine and marijuana dependence and poly substance abuse. This program was Rick's fourth attempt at sobriety, which included two inpatient facilities (one in Brazil and one in the United States) and a 1-year period of outpatient therapy in conjunction with attendance at Narcotics Anonymous (also in the United States). Rick presented to our facility at the request of his mother, who stated that this was her "last attempt at helping him to get straight." Rick had been unemployed for 14 months prior to his admittance and had been living with friends for the last 9 months. He recently was asked to leave his friend's home as a result of a dispute over money and had been sleeping on the street for the last 2 weeks. In contacting his mother for assistance, Rick was told that the only way that she would help was if he would "check himself into rehab and get rid of the drugs." Rick presented as disheveled and depressed, stating this was his last resort and "this time I'm serious."

Rick began using alcohol and cigarettes at the age of 9, advanced to marijuana use at age 11, marijuana abuse by age 12, and dependence at age 14 (daily use). Rick has been smoking marijuana steadily since age 14. He began using cocaine at the age of 17 and quickly progressed to dependency by age 18. His longest period of abstinence from cocaine was 9 months, which corresponded to his time in outpatient therapy.

Rick was born and raised into a culturally mixed household in São Paulo, Brazil. His father, James, was a Caucasian American enlisted in the United States Army at the time that Rick was born. His mother, Andrea (a native Brazilian), was born and raised in São Paulo. Rick was the eldest of three children. The next oldest male, Juan, was 4 years his junior. The baby sister, Clarita, was 8 years his junior. His father stayed with the family until Rick was 9 years old and then abruptly left Brazil for the United States. Rick remained with his mother and younger siblings until he was 16, at which time he requested to move to the United States to live with his father. Having dealt with Rick's behavioral problems since he was 9 years of age, his mother readily agreed to the move in the hopes of providing Rick with some discipline. Rick stayed with his father, who according to Rick "had a big drinking problem" for 2 years and finished high school by completing his GED. At 19, Rick enlisted in the Army but was discharged after 3 months when cocaine was found in his system as a result of a random urinalysis. Since that time, Rick has held a variety of jobs, including working as a carpenter's apprentice, a waiter, a bartender, and a limousine driver. He was fired from his last position, driving a limousine, as a result of a DUI (cocaine). Since that time, Rick has been unemployed.

Incident

Rick was assigned to me as his counselor while living and working at the residential treatment facility. He had been making satisfactory progress in his recovery program and had maintained 6 months of continued sobriety, as evidenced by both self-report and periodic urinalyses. Treatment initially consisted of 8 hours of day treatment per day, 1 hour of individual counseling per week, and three group counseling sessions per week. After 3 months, Rick was assisted with securing employment in a sober environment while maintaining his individual and group counseling schedules. It was during his 6th month of treatment that Rick made a breakthrough in his recovery during an individual session.

Rick shared two separate (yet related) concerns. First, he stated that he had been experiencing problems at work, namely arriving late and appearing lethargic while on the job. Second, Rick revealed that he had been experiencing increased self-loathing and shame. In a holistic assessment of Rick's current situation, he shared that he was averaging approximately 4 hours of sleep per night during the workweek. This led to a discussion of what was occupying his time at night, leading him to share (with a great deal of hesitation and shame) that he had been spending an average of 3 to 4 hours per night on the Internet looking at, and acting out to, pornography. This led to a further discussion regarding the source of his shame and self-loathing. Rick revealed that the majority of his time was spent looking at sites that highlighted hard-core pornographic acts with older women, something that he considered to be "weird." This led me to do a thorough sexual history and assessment in our two following individual sessions in an attempt to determine both the source of his arousal patterns and whether he was experiencing sexual addiction.

During our next session, Rick revealed that he was introduced to sex at the very young age of 5. He shared that it is a common practice in many South American countries for the hired servants to introduce male children to the realities of sex and sexual intercourse. Typical of many families, Rick's parents had two live-in maids that cleaned, cooked, and provided child care for the family. At age 5, Rick recalled one of the maids being sexually inappropriate (i.e., fondling his genitals) with him on a regular basis during his bath time.

Critical Incidents in Addictions Counseling

This proceeded until Rick was 9, the age at which he lost his virginity with another maid. Rick continued to be very sexually active throughout his childhood and adolescence and encountered pornography for the first time at age 11 when he happened across an old collection of his father's magazines that had been stored away. Throughout his adolescence and early adulthood, Rick continued using pornography and masturbation on a regular basis, anywhere from daily use to three to four times per week. He has had numerous (approximately 40+) female sexual partners, many of them anonymous "one-night stands," had engaged in sexual acts with prostitutes on at least 15 occasions, and has often frequented adult entertainment facilities (bookstores, topless bars, etc.). It was not until checking into our facility that Rick had constant access to the Internet, so he believed that his current sexual activities on the Internet have been an easy substitute for the other behaviors that are currently against our facility's rules and regulations. Compulsive (i.e., at least once a day) masturbation has been a mainstay in Rick's life since early adolescence.

For our next session, I assessed Rick for the presence of sexual addiction using a structured interview based on the acronym *WASTE Time*. Similar to the development of the CAGE clinical interview developed by Ewing and Rouse in 1970 (Ewing, 1984) to assess for alcohol dependence, I developed the WASTE Time acronym/informal assessment instrument based on the diagnostic criteria for sexual addiction. Given my work with sexually addicted clients in the past, I felt that "the designation of this particular acronym seemed appropriate given the tremendous amounts of wasted time that most sexually addicted clients admit to in the pursuit of their sexual behaviors" (Hagedorn & Juhnke, in press). The letters forming this acronym represent particular diagnostic criteria that have been developed for sexual addiction (Goodman, 2001) and are asked during the structured interview to gather appropriate data. Similar to the CAGE, I have found that those clients who answer affirmatively to one of the questions typically exhibit symptomatology indicating a strong possibility for the presence of sexual addiction. Further assessment is warranted for these clients as well as an intervention by a trained counselor. For clients who answer affirmatively to two or more questions, a high probability of sexual addiction is indicated, warranting immediate intervention by a trained counselor. Following are the bolded questions (found in Hagedorn & Juhnke, in press) I asked (I left out any elaboration for the sake of brevity) during the structured interview and Rick's italicized (and truncated) responses:

> **W–Withdrawal:** "Have you experienced any withdrawal symptoms when you are unable to engage in sexual activities?"
> *Yeah, I get moody and can't concentrate. Sometimes I get nervous when I'm around other people . . . plus, I tend to blow up pretty easy at work if I haven't had my "release" the night before.*
>
> **A–Adverse Consequences:** "Have you experienced any negative or adverse consequences as a result of your sexual behaviors?"
> *Well, I'm not getting enough sleep for one. Also, Manny [his boss] has been riding me pretty hard at work because I tend to drift off. . . . oh, and the other day*

Jesse [the house manager—Rick lives in a group home] *saw what I was looking at and took away my computer privileges for a week, but what he doesn't know won't hurt him.*

S–Inability to Stop: "Have you attempted to cut back, control, or stop your sexual behaviors without success?"

I tell myself, "Okay, I'm just gonna check my email for 15 minutes and then I'm gonna go crash." Before I know it, it's like 3 o'clock in the morning. I haven't really thought about stopping, other than it might get me in trouble. . . .

T–Tolerance or Intensity: "Have you found it necessary to increase the amount or intensity of your sexual behaviors to achieve the same effect?"

At first I was looking at the "Sports Illustrated" swimsuit issues on line 'cause I didn't think others would consider that breaking one of the rules. The other guys even joined in with me. Then I started "browsing" past some of the soft-core porn, you know, like topless sites even though I know that's against the rules. But that wasn't doing it for me. Now I'm always looking for that perfect hard-core site or picture—that's what takes me so long at night.

E–Escape: "Do you use sexual activity as an escape from negative mood states, such as stress, anxiety, depression, sadness, or anger?"

It's not like being in rehab is my favorite thing. . . . Sure, I get bummed about being here and about the way my life is, but like that Billy Joel song, I like to get online and "forget about life for a while."

Time–Time Spent (preparing, engaging, or recovering) or Time Wasted: "Have you found yourself spending a lot of time preparing for, engaging in, or recovering from a sexual activity?"

I guess so, I mean I gotta wait until everyone else is in bed and asleep, then I sneak out and log on, then I search and search for just the right thing. By the time I'm done, I feel wasted. This has been going on for something like 5 months or so. . . .

"Have you been spending more time and/or more resources on your sexual activities than you intended?"

If you count sleep as resources, then sure, I've been losing a lot of that.

Given the guidelines provided at the beginning of this dialogue, I determined that Rick met sufficient criteria for sexual addiction. Given that this was the end of our session, my homework suggestion for the following week was that Rick think about attending a local meeting of SAA (Sex Addicts Anonymous) with some of the other clients who attend from our facility. Rick agreed with the suggestion.

Rick returned the following week with new insight and awareness of his addictive patterns. Over the next few sessions, we used both what Rick had learned in the SAA meetings and the model developed by Carnes (1994), known as the Addictive System, to explore his belief system, impaired thought processes, and sense of unmanageability, as well as his cycle of obsessive thought patterns, ritualistic behaviors, acting out, and resulting despair. Rick continued to display increased insight and self-understanding into how his sexual activities met the same need for a "high" as did his chemical use.

Discussion

Perhaps one of the most significant events of Rick's therapy was his association between his chemical and process addictions. Without prompting, Rick was the first to suggest that his sexually addictive acts went hand in hand with his use of marijuana and cocaine. He was able to associate how his being under the influence of chemicals both helped to arouse his sexual appetite and softened the self-loathing and shame that often resulted. With further exploration, Rick shared that he still held on to a lot of anger, directed primarily at women, for how he had been molested as a boy. This anger, coupled with the shame he felt when he engaged in sexual acts, which he believed to be immoral or "weird," helped to fuel his need for chemical relief. Additionally, Rick was able to recognize that most of his relapses into chemical use and addiction followed a negative cycle of sexual addiction.

To conclude, Rick once shared the following insight: "Giving up pot and coke has been a 'breeze' compared to giving up the addictive sex—I mean, it's everywhere. I don't have to call up my friend or dealer to get a dime bag; all I gotta do is log on and I'm in la-la land. It's crazy!" For Rick, then, addictive sex needed to be addressed before, or at the very least in conjunction with, his chemical dependency. For him, and many other addicts, addictive sex is the last to go.

Questions

1. For Rick, addictive sexual patterns developed either before, or in conjunction with, addictive chemical use. I have found this pattern to be increasingly more common among the clients with whom I work. How important is it to conduct a thorough addictive history, to include process addictions (e.g., sex, gambling, food, Internet use, spending) with every chemically addicted client?
   a. What kind of assessment(s)/structured interview(s) would you use to assess for the presence of multiple addictions?
   b. What comorbid addictive disorders do you believe are more common among males? Among females? Among different age groups, ethnic groups, sexual orientations?
2. What comes first, the chicken or the egg? That is, do you believe process addictive patterns occur first, or does chemical use/misuse happen earlier? Do they occur together?
3. Based on your response to Question 2, what does this mean for prevention strategies?
4. Should all addictions be treated with a similar model? Which one would work best?
5. Should all addictions be treated at the same time, or should they be addressed separately?

■Response

Joseph P. Jordan

This case is an excellent example of problems faced by dually addicted (chemical and process addicted) clients. While dual addiction has been treated within the field of alcohol and other drug (AOD) abuse treatment for many years, it is usually associated with people addicted to alcohol and some other intoxicating agent, such as benzodiazepines or opiates. It is only within the last decade that I have seen the problems of sexual addiction, gambling, spending, or other process addictions identified as addictive disorder that occur in conjunction with chemical addictions such as alcohol, cocaine, or other substances.

As this clinician points out in Question 1, Rick's sexual abuse and compulsive behavior happened both prior to and in conjunction with his chemical abuse. Just as AOD addiction has been acknowledged as a process, so may sexual addiction be characterized as a process, one with precursor conditions, a course of development, and identifiable symptoms. Therefore, it would be vital to have a comprehensive sexual behavior history such as the one described in this scenario. Indeed, without gathering such a detailed history of clients, it is impossible to develop appropriate treatment interventions. Initial assessment shapes initial treatment, and ongoing assessment shapes ongoing treatment. Accordingly, I would consider a thorough psychosocial assessment that focuses especially on areas of compulsive behavior to be paramount in the initial treatment interventions of any client referred for chemical dependency counseling.

I would note here that while almost all addicts are compulsive in areas, this does not necessarily mean they meet the criteria for having a process addiction. I have treated many cocaine addicts who have described compulsive behavior with regard to sex or money, but not all of them were experiencing dual process and chemical addictions. Accordingly, as is pointed out in this scenario, it is important to utilize clinical assessment skills to determine the extent of the client's process addiction, if one exists at all.

In response to Question 1, Part a, I would recommend a combination approach to assessment of compulsive behaviors and AOD addictions, meaning I would combine my assessment of chemical and process addictions. Because of the nature of dual addictions, they often manifest at the same point in time. For example, a cocaine addict may engage in behavior that is typical of sexual addiction such as cruising for prostitutes while under the influence of cocaine, whereas an alcoholic may gamble while intoxicated. Therefore, by asking clarifying questions about the nature of someone's AOD use, such as, "So where were you when you were last under the influence of cocaine?—*Cruising around downtown*" or "What do you normally do when you are drinking?—*Playing cards with my buddies*," I can listen carefully for clues to whether my client might be engaging in other addictions. Then, should such clues exist, I would encourage further elaboration by the client so as to determine whether these other process addiction behaviors meet criteria for abuse or dependence. As always, the *Diagnostic and Statistical Manual of Mental Disorders* (4th ed., Text Revision; *DSM-IV-TR*) of the American Psychiatric Association (2000) provides appropriate guidelines for what constitutes abuse or dependence.

Of particular interest to me in this scenario is the use of a mnemonic device to aid in the assessment of sexual addiction (WASTE Time). Mnemonic devices have been used in the assessment of AOD addiction for many years

(CAGE—**C**ontrol drinking, **A**nger when confronted, **G**uilt over use, "**E**ye-opener" [Ewing, 1984]; BUMP—**B**lackouts, **U**nplanned use, **M**ore than intended, **P**re use before social events), and they are often invaluable in helping clinicians identify red flags for further assessment of a client's chemical use. What is particularly interesting about this device is the incorporation of withdrawal and tolerance (**WASTE**) into the device. These two are what I like to call "alarm bells"; if they are ringing, I begin looking very hard to find where the addiction is hiding. Therefore, while this mnemonic device is still under development, I would encourage clinicians to develop and utilize such tools to aid them in the recognition of addictive disorders.

In regard to Question 1, Part b, in which this clinician asks whether I have observed particular addictions associated with different genders, ethnic groups, or sexual orientations, I would respond by stating emphatically that addiction is a disorder that crosses all lines. If years of treating addictive disorders have taught me anything, it has been to never assume that addictions will stay within categories of any kind, cultural or otherwise. That being said, most of the clients I have treated with a combination of AOD and process addictions have been male, Caucasian, between the ages of 25 and 55, and equally heterosexual and homosexual. Additionally, I have observed that during inpatient chemical dependency treatment episodes, more men than women will present for sexual addiction and AOD addiction treatment. However, I believe this to be a function of the fact that more men than women present for inpatient treatment of AOD addiction, therefore women may not feel as comfortable in admitting or addressing their chemical and sexual addiction issues while being a minority of the treatment milieu. As it was in the beginning of alcoholism treatment, female alcoholics presented for treatment at far lower rates than those of male alcoholics; I expect the same is going on with process addictions and minority groups. Therefore, while I believe process addictions occur with the same frequency within all people, I also believe that barriers for effective process addiction treatment keep minority groups from presenting for treatment. Additionally, process addiction treatment is still very new, and I know of no treatment paradigms that address the cultural needs of minorities. Therefore, current treatment paradigms for process addictions may not be appropriate for minority clients.

Responding to Question 2, whether the process addiction or the AOD addiction occurs first, is difficult in some cases and impossible in most. One might point to the process addiction behavior precursors that occurred at age 5 for Rick. These behaviors occurred long before his use of cigarettes and alcohol at age 9. However, this sexual behavior is abusive in nature (an adult maid who fondled Rick while bathing him) and certainly created maladaptive beliefs concerning sexual behavior, just as Rick's first use of cigarettes and alcohol was inappropriate in nature (beginning both at age 9) and created maladaptive beliefs concerning use of drugs and alcohol. Did Rick use to deal with his sexual abuse or did Rick sexually act out when under the influence? Who is to say that Rick's use of alcohol and drugs did not further exacerbate his sexual addiction, or even serve a causal function?

Sexual Addiction as a Precursor to Chemical Addiction

What is most important is that dual addictions cannot be treated separately. Therefore, to answer the question as to which came first is useless for the therapist and may even be counterproductive for the client. Early recovery is a difficult time for clients and is often characterized by concrete and either/or thinking. Identification of a "first" addiction may encourage an early recovery client (concrete thinking) to only treat the "primary" addiction, which inevitably creates the opportunity for a relapse in the "second" addiction. Therefore, clinicians must help clients to see the dual nature of their addictions and the necessity to treat both at the same time. I would liken this to the issue of co-occurring disorders such as depression and alcoholism. Treat one exclusively, and you risk your client relapsing with the other issue.

As far as Question 3, I am not yet aware of any prevention strategies exclusively for process addictions. However, as was pointed out in my response to Question 2, it is vital to treat process and AOD addictions at the same time. Therefore, prevention efforts for chemical addictions would possibly work with process addictions, especially if a strengths-based approach is used rather than an educationally based approach. Most of the successful prevention programs currently in use focus on building children's self-esteem, self-worth, confidence, and refusal skills (i.e., strengths necessary to refuse drugs or alcohol). My work with dual AOD and process addiction clients has led me to believe that the precursor feelings and conditions for one addiction also took them to another addiction. Therefore, if prevention works for one addiction, it would work for another, provided it builds individuals' self-esteem and teaches them to value themselves in ways that make them less likely to look outside themselves (e.g., drugs, alcohol, sex, gambling) for happiness.

Question 4 asks whether all addictions should be treated with a similar model. I believe there is a particular model appropriate for treatment of addictions, AOD, or process, called the bio-psycho-socio-spiritual model of addiction. As one can imagine from the name, this model addresses the biological, psychological, sociological, and spiritual causes of addiction, as well as calling for treatment in these areas. It is a holistic model that gives the clinician a framework whereby he or she might explore the multiple components of a client's addictive disorders. Additionally, by calling attention to the multifaceted nature of the client's addictive disorder(s), the clinician is then more easily able to facilitate multiple interventions for the client in a variety of areas (i.e., physical, social, psychological). This is due to the client's acceptance of his or her addictive disorder(s) as having biological, psychological, sociological, and spiritual components, thereby necessitating interventions in all of the aforementioned areas.

Question 5 asks whether process and chemical addictions should be treated separately or at the same time. To answer this question, I am going to pose a question in response: If a patient came into an emergency room with a broken arm and having an asthma attack, would the appropriate course of treatment be to treat the broken arm first and deal with the asthma later, or vice versa? Of course not. To do so would be ludicrous. As previously mentioned, one would not dream of treating only the alcoholism of someone with co-occurring disorders of depression and alcoholism. It would set the client up for relapse on whatever disorder was excluded from treatment. In my experience as a clinician, multiple addictions, process or otherwise, must be addressed during treatment if the client is to enjoy a lasting and comfortable sobriety.

It is my hope that a thoroughly comprehensive assessment for the presence of process addictions becomes a standard part of AOD abuse assessments. Too many times I have seen the damage caused by untreated gambling, sex, Internet, shopping, or other process addictions on a newly recovering person's life, resulting in the person's return to active AOD use and even more acting out with his or her process addiction. No longer can the field of AOD abuse counseling ignore process addictions with attitudes such as "Just treat the alcohol and drugs; the rest will take care of itself" or "Chemicals first; lifestyle second." Examples such as the above case show how competent counselors trained to recognize and treat process addictions are a necessity in the field of addictions counseling. If we fail to recognize this, we fail both the field of addictions counseling and our clients, both of whom deserve our best efforts. Therefore, I can only hope that, as a field, addictions counselors will seek the necessary knowledge and skills to become proficient process addiction counselors.

■References

American Psychiatric Association. (2000). *Diagnostic and statistical manual of mental disorders* (4th ed., Text Revision). Washington, DC: Author.

Carnes, P. (1994). *Contrary to love: Helping the sexual addict.* Center City, MN: Hazelden.

Ewing, J. A. (1984). Detecting alcoholism. *Journal of the American Medical Association, 252,* 1905–1907.

Goodman, A. (2001). What's in a name? Terminology for designating a syndrome of driven sexual behavior. *Sexual Addiction & Compulsivity, 8,* 191–213.

Hagedorn, W. B., & Juhnke, G. A. (in press). Treating the sexually addicted client: Establishing a need for increased counselor awareness. *Journal of Addictions & Offender Counseling.*

5
Group Addictions Interventions

■Critical Incident

Marcheta P. Evans

Background

Marie was a 55-year-old African American female from a large, southern city. She was referred to my practice to participate in an ongoing addictions group counseling experience with multicultural emphases. The referral occurred after Marie's discharge from a 30-day, voluntary hospitalization. Marie was admitted for this hospitalization following a Loritab overdose. During our initial visit, Marie disclosed that she was also taking prescribed medications of Lustral and Tussionex to relieve her depression and her allergy-related cough.

Approximately 1 year ago, Marie was critically injured in a serious car accident. Another driver forced her off the road while she was returning home from a late dinner with some friends. She sustained several fractures in her arms and legs, suffered internal injuries, and was in severe pain even after numerous surgeries. She reported being depressed because of the pain and immobilization caused by the accident. Concomitantly, she had feelings of failure and guilt related to an earlier divorce.

Her medical doctors prescribed several types of pain medications to assist with her pain management. However, the Loritab seemed to be Marie's prescription of choice. One physician prescribed Lustral to assist with her lethargy/depression, and another prescribed Tussionex to provide relief from a persistent cough.

Additional background information included the fact that Marie was employed as an information technology systems manager for a telecommunications company. She was the oldest of six children, and both of her parents continued to live in the city where Marie was born. An area of interest noted during Marie's intake was her emphasis on her biological family. When asked the question "Tell me about who you are?" Marie immediately proceeded to describe her mother and father. She became very animated when she described her father as a senior minister at one of the oldest and most prominent Baptist churches in the city. He was very active in the civil rights movement and had marched with Martin Luther King Jr. during several of the boycotts in the South during the 1960s. When she described her mother, she smiled and stated, "Mother was the rock for the children and father." Marie reported her mother as having been the primary emotional support of the family. She continued by describing her family as extremely religious and conservative with a strong belief in God, family, purpose, values, service, and community.

When questions were posed regarding her immediate family, Marie stated that she was a divorced mother of three daughters. She divorced approximately 6 years ago from her husband of 30 years. Marie reported that she married when she was "very young and naive." Marie further stated, "I just wanted to make a good Christian home for my children and husband. You know, I wanted a fairy-tale home with a happy ending. But, that was not to be for me." Marie indicated her divorce centered on her husband's infidelity and his strong opinion that Marie was too religious. All three of Marie's daughters were grown and lived away from home. The two younger daughters were college graduates, and the oldest daughter was "still struggling to figure out what she wants to do with her life."

When Marie was asked about previous counseling, she reported participating with her husband in Christian-based couples counseling sessions while she was going through her divorce. However, Marie expressed that counseling was contrary to what her family of origin values: "You should turn your problems over to God and let Him solve them." Marie stated that she felt guilty and had major doubts about seeking professional help, especially in light of the overdose that had led to her prior psychiatric hospitalization. She reported, "Maybe I don't have enough faith or I'm not trusting God like I should." Reportedly these thoughts were constantly swirling through her mind as she pondered her participation in the group counseling experience.

Incident

During our first addictions group counseling session, Marie disclosed feelings of helplessness and hopelessness. She indicated that these feelings had continued even after her release from her most recent hospitalization. During group, Marie continued to express deep-seated feelings of failure as a wife. She indicated that her "failure" as a wife would negatively affect her daughters. Additional concerns centered on her continued abuse and dependence on pain medication and antidepressants. It should be further noted that Marie had specifically requested a Christian African American female counselor and was originally reticent to join the group counseling experience.

During our first group session, Marie repeatedly expressed concern regarding her present condition by stating, "How could I have ended up like this—addicted and depressed?" She adamantly denied any intent to commit suicide and reported the reason she had previously attempted suicide was because "The pain was so unbearable." Marie appropriately interacted with other group members and reportedly was "relieved" to have an opportunity to honestly express herself. At the conclusion of the session, she stated to the counselor that it was "nice" to be able to join a group of Christian African American females "like me." Prior to our first counseling session, Marie indicated that she had previously had difficulty talking to others, especially in the hospital, because of what she perceived was their inability to understand her issues from a religious and cultural perspective.

During our third group counseling experience, one of the other members indicated that Marie should just "get over" her previous divorce and quit "sabotaging" her recovery by placing her abstinence in God's hands. Marie broke into tears and indicated that her faith in God would get her through her recovery: "Jesus will get me through." Another group member challenged Marie, indicating, "Well, he hasn't gotten you through it yet! And you haven't stopped using." Despite my best efforts to keep Marie in the group, she discontinued group counseling shortly after the fourth session. During my later telephone calls, Marie continued to deny suicidal thoughts and agreed to contact the local help-line number if she felt overwhelmed or felt like hurting or killing herself. However, she never returned to group.

Discussion

Approximately 1 year after Marie's leaving the group, she reappeared at the agency and indicated that she was doing well. She reported to her former counselor that her depression had "lifted" and that she had begun dating again. Concomitantly, she noted that her use of "all" medications and substances had stopped and that "God was smiling" on her again.

Questions

1. Understanding and integrating the importance of culture in Marie's case, do you believe that group counseling was an inappropriate counseling modality for this client?
2. How might I have used Marie's sense of faith and religion as greater resources to her recovery and her experience in the group?
3. Might family counseling have been a better counseling modality with this client?
4. Given that Marie had specifically requested a "Christian African American female counselor," might it have been more appropriate to encourage her participation with others from different religious and ethnic backgrounds?
5. Given her previous suicide attempt and her reported feelings of hopelessness and helplessness, besides continuing to contact her, are there other things that I could have suggested to ensure that she not suicide?

■Response

Larry Golden

I am thankful to the author for presenting this challenge. It would have been easy enough to present a slam-dunk case. Instead, the author provides a case in which her client, Marie, dropped out of counseling altogether. For the most part, the questions I will respond to reflect the counselor's interest in figuring out this all too common and unsatisfying outcome. With the glorious benefit of hindsight, I will do my best.

In the first question, the counselor asks, "Understanding and integrating the importance of culture in Marie's case, do you believe that group counseling was an inappropriate counseling modality for this client?"

Group counseling offers affirmation and support that cannot be had in individual therapy. Of course, confrontation is an inevitable occurrence in group work, especially with addictions, and there is no way to guarantee that the confrontation will be gentle.

After the first group session, Marie said she felt relieved to have expressed her feelings. In the session, she identified nicely with this group of Christian African American females. But during the third session, when Marie said, "Jesus will get me through," another group member countered with, "He hasn't gotten you through it yet! And you haven't stopped using." Marie dropped out after the fourth session without offering any explanation. It is very possible that she did not like being confronted.

The second question is, "How might I have used Marie's sense of faith and religion as greater resources to her recovery and her experience in the group?" Given Marie's pervasive distrust of counseling, a secular counselor may be at a disadvantage. On the other hand, Marie's abiding faith creates an opening for a counselor with fundamental Christian credentials. A client like Marie is God's gift to a pastoral counselor. It really is time for the antagonism between psychotherapy and organized religion to end. I think that most secular counselors today acknowledge that religion is a positive force in the lives of many clients.

The third question asks, "Might family counseling have been a better counseling modality with this client?" This question brings out my own strong bias that family counseling is the way to go, always, *unless* family members are unavailable or outright dangerous. I really have no way of knowing whether Marie's family was willing or able to participate.

The fourth question asks, "Given that Marie had specifically requested a "Christian African American female counselor," might it have been more appropriate to encourage her participation with others from different religious and ethnic backgrounds?"

I suspect that underneath this question, the counselor is expressing her own conviction that a fully functioning person in 21st-century America should be able to interact with others of all races and cultures. Nevertheless, the counselor honored Marie's request for a female African American counselor and placed her in a group of African American women. From a constructivist perspective, counselors must honor the client's wisdom, and I am pleased that the counselor did so.

Here is the counselor's fifth and final question: "Given her previous suicide attempt and her reported feelings of hopelessness and helplessness, besides continuing to contact her, are there other things that I could have suggested to ensure that she not suicide?"

The counselor phoned after Marie dropped out of counseling and Marie denied suicidal ideation and agreed to contact the local help-line, if the need arose. I cannot think of what else can be done in the case of an adult client. I will assume that the counselor has carefully documented her efforts so that she can defend herself in the event of a suicide.

6
Addictions Prevention and Intervention Within Schools

■Critical Incident

Virginia A. Kelly

Background

I have been a middle school counselor at the same school for approximately 8 years. The school is located in a small rural community. The three counselors divide students by grade. Then, each of us follows one student group from sixth through eighth grades. This system allows me to focus on issues relevant to a specific grade over the course of an academic year. For example, when I get a new group of sixth graders, I am able to focus on adjustment to middle school issues in a more intensive fashion.

One of the groups I have come to define as critical is what I call my "potential high-risk group." When I have a group of sixth graders, I ask the teachers, toward the end of the school year, to identify students they feel are at high risk for using drugs. Then, at the start of the seventh grade, I interview these identified students and begin developing groups as a preventive measure. I have developed a 10-week group for seventh graders. The group covers a variety of drug use and abuse topics. I generally try to limit the group to eight members. Over the years, I have run as many as five of these over the course of the year. I eventually implemented an "after-care" program as well. This program runs once a week, after school hours. This component resembles a student 12-step meeting and provides ongoing support in the form of weekly meetings.

Over the years the number of students identified as high risk has sharply increased. Last year, teachers requested that I allow 70 students to participate in my group. More specifically, I have noticed (albeit anecdotally) that the nature and quality of issues that surface within the group setting have become increasingly more serious. The number of students experimenting with substances other than marijuana and alcohol has grown exponentially. Furthermore, the co-occurrence of other behaviors and seemingly diagnosable issues (e.g., cutting, depression, eating disorders) has risen.

Incident

A case that I had during this past school year was typical of this phenomenon. Predictably, I had far too many students to include in a single high-risk group. I therefore asked teachers to prioritize the needs as they saw fit. I wound up running two groups of eight students each during October of last year. In one group I had five male and three female students, all in the seventh grade. I had one honors student who was very involved in the life of the school, two athletes who were highly involved in their sports, three students who were average students who seemed moderately connected to school in ways other than those associated with academic performance, and three students who were struggling academically and were "hanging on by a thread" in terms of their commitment to and connection with the school community. The student I would like to focus on is one of the athletes.

Specifically, Shar was a solid B student who was a track star. She had begun to run track the previous year; up until that time, she had not identified herself as a student athlete. During sixth grade she discovered that she not only was fast but also had tremendous endurance, which allowed her to run long distances. Initially, this newly found talent seemed a positive attribute, allowing this slightly above-average student to excel. However, after several months of "stardom," Shar began to exhibit behavioral changes that concerned her teachers.

Shar had always been fairly quiet. Prior to middle school she might have been described as an "easy" student to have in a classroom. She was a good student, her behaviors were typical for her developmental level, and she was well liked by other students. However, toward the end of sixth grade, her grades dropped dramatically; she barely passed the final marking period. Her teachers also noted a change in her classroom behaviors; she seemed to vacillate between listlessness and agitation that frequently resulted in behavioral outbursts that could not be controlled in the classroom setting.

When I got involved with Shar, in the beginning of her seventh-grade year, she was somewhat hostile and angry and denied that there were any problems associated with her behavior. I was, however, successful in obtaining her agreement to attend my group.

Initially, Shar was quiet in the group. As we got to know each other and began to explore information related to drugs and their effects, Shar was reticent and slow to share on a personal level. Over several weeks, other group members began to disclose the nature of their own use, but Shar remained noticeably silent. However, during the fourth meeting of the group, one of the other students confronted Shar. At the first signs of confrontation, Shar became almost violently defensive. However, she did not retreat entirely and eventually wound up in tears. In a highly emotional outpouring, Shar revealed that she had been using OxyContin for almost a year and that she was addicted. OxyContin is a prescription painkiller in the opiate family. As such, the nature of its addictive qualities compares closely with that of heroin. It is actually assumed that OxyContin is more addictive than heroin and may initiate more serious and life-threatening withdrawal symptoms. According to law enforcement statistics, the abuse of OxyContin among adolescents has increased dramatically, initiating legal action and the refusal of a variety of pharmacies to stock the drug.

In tears, Shar shared with the group her initial exposure to OxyContin and almost immediate addiction to the substance. She stated that she had tried repeatedly to stop using the drug with no hint of success. She felt hopeless and expressed deep fear related to ever being drug free again.

Discussion

This kind of a disclosure by a seventh-grade student in a rural, fairly isolated school is rare, especially in a group setting. I knew that I had to deal with this issue in a careful manner so as to protect Shar and deal with the feelings and possible subsequent behavior of the remainder of the group. Initially, I chose to be as honest as I could with the group. I acknowledged that this was a very upsetting and serious issue. We processed the shock of the group, and I allowed students to express fears and concerns, most of which were presented in the form of love and support for Shar. I reminded group members of our commitment to confidentiality, knowing that this would be a very difficult commitment for many of them to keep. I made arrangements for the group to meet the next day and told group members that they could stop by sooner if they felt the need to do so. I was then left with Shar.

The issues of "duty to warn" and breaching confidentiality are always complex and become even more so when presented with adolescent drug use issues. We know that we have both legal and ethical responsibilities to disclose information when we suspect that a client is at risk of harming him- or herself or others. What has yet to be determined at a functional level is how this relates to experimentation with substances among the adolescent population. Do I, as a school counselor, disclose every incident of drug and alcohol use that I am aware of? If I know that there was a party last Saturday night where marijuana and alcohol were present, do I "tell"? Do I tell if I know the party was at a senior's house? What if the party was at the house of a sixth grader? Where do I draw that line? These questions provide much fodder for conversation and disagreement among school counselors everywhere.

However, in the case of Shar, the issue of disclosure was clear. I told Shar that she was very brave and that she had made a huge step in her recovery by disclosing her OxyContin use to the group. I also tried to reassure her that there was help and that I would assist her in accessing it. I spoke with her for approximately a half hour before I broached the subject of disclosure.

When I let her know that I needed to go further with this information, Shar seemed to understand. She was not surprised by this information and seemed resigned to my calling her parents and telling the school administration what had transpired. I called the principal into our meeting and disclosed Shar's substance use. The principal called Shar's parents, and I waited with her until they arrived at the school. I met with Shar's parents and shared the information I had. I was also able to share specific information regarding both opiate addiction and local treatment facilities. I suggested that they immediately take Shar to the local emergency room and contact treatment facilities that might provide options for the next step in what was bound to become a long and complicated process.

Questions

1. How involved should a school counselor be once a case like this is handed over to a treatment facility?
2. What is the best way to process this incident with the remainder of the group?
3. What is the role of the school counselor in terms of reintegrating a student like Shar back into the school environment upon completion of treatment? What kinds of supports and resources should be in place at that point?

■Response

Gerald A. Juhnke

Let me commend the counselor on the innovative and dedicated efforts used. This counselor clearly has a heart for students. The prevention and treatment experiences provided by the counselor are quite admirable. Based on what has been reported, it seems likely that the students perceive the counselor as being committed and helpful to them. Thus, continued support and involvement—especially while students are in the transferring and beginning stages of treatment elsewhere—seems key to successful treatment. As a matter of fact, the counselor's continued involvement and support provides a transitional "bridge" for students both entering treatment and—once discharged—returning to school.

It has been my experience that youths entering treatment are often anxious. A known and trusted counselor such as the individual described, who has an ongoing relationship with the client, can help her make a solid connection with the new, unknown, external treatment providers. Concomitantly, the knowledge the counselor has gained about the client during the group experiences can help ensure that the agency to which the youth is referred fully understands the client's immediate needs, strengths, and supports. Of course, one could not share this information without appropriate releases. However, it would seem Shar and her parents would welcome concerted efforts to make the student's transition into the new treatment agency as easy and unencumbered as possible. Additionally, when it is time for the student to be released or to reenter the school, the counselor will be a vital resource. For example, students reentering school following detoxification and hospitalization would likely benefit from additional support in the form of referral for special education services. The counselor's expertise and understanding of the school (e.g., placement procedures, faculty, the students' previous relationships with other substance-abusing and recovering students within the school, policies, and available resources) and addictions counseling make this professional a critical component to successful school reintegration.

On the basis of my group experiences with younger alcohol and other drug (AOD) abusing clients, I might use parts of an adapted debriefing model (Juhnke, 2000). Specifically, I would begin by asking group members who were present when Shar admitted her OxyContin addiction the following question: "What was your first thought when you heard Shar say she was addicted to OxyContin?" The purpose of this question is twofold. First, it allows students a nonthreatening way to process Shar's admission. Specifically, this question asks students to report what they "think" versus what they "feel" about Shar's addiction. In other words, it encourages students to think about what happened rather than experience any potential overwhelming feelings. The question also provides students a forum within a safe group experience to discuss what it was like to learn that a peer was addicted. Thus, students can indicate their concerns for Shar. Second, the question allows students an opportunity to discuss their anxiety and fears related to their own substance abuse or addictions.

The follow-up to this question might be something like, "What was the most scary or difficult thing you have experienced as a result of Shar's statement regarding her being addicted?" This question encourages students to move from the first question's cognitive realm to a feelings-oriented realm. Thus, students have the freedom of discussing their feelings related to Shar's addiction, their addiction, or addiction in general. Addicted students I have counseled often talk about their fears. These fears generally revolve around two areas: their fear that they are addicted or their fear that they have "lost control" of their lives as a result of their cravings and the behaviors they must continue to purchase drugs (e.g., theft, prostitution).

Depending on the outcomes of the first two questions, I might then provide students with a handout describing substance abuse and addiction symptoms. Additionally, I might ask students if they have ever experienced any of these symptoms and encourage their participation in an addictions assessment. I have even found it helpful to use a question like, "Given that many people are afraid to ask for help, what things could we do to let fellow members know that we are willing to help them should they be concerned that they are addicted?" This question's purpose is to help group members describe how they might help others and to promote mutual caretaking within the group.

It is clear that school counselors play a vital role in the reintegration of a student like Shar into the school milieu. This can be facilitated by participating in potential Individualized Education Plan (IEP) meetings upon Shar's return, initiating individual counseling sessions, scheduling "check-in meetings" to determine Shar's progress, and asking Shar about experienced relapses or feared upcoming stressors that may promote relapse. Additionally, the school counselor can talk with the group regarding how they can welcome Shar back into the group before Shar's return. Support cards and letters to Shar from group prior to Shar's program completion would likely be welcomed. Other supports and resources for Shar and her family might include 12-step programs such as Alateen and Al-Anon as well as family counseling sessions.

■Reference

Juhnke, G. A. (2000). *Addressing school violence: Practical strategies and interventions.* Greensboro, NC: ERIC/CASS.

Critical Incidents in Addictions Counseling

7
Spirituality and Addictions Counseling

■Critical Incident

James O. Fuller

Background

Richard is a 50-year-old male who has struggled with substance abuse and addictions issues since he was in high school, although he had experienced symptoms of agitation and low self-esteem during his elementary and middle school years. Because of bouts of depression during his teens, he began using alcohol, tobacco, hallucinogenic drugs, amphetamines, and pornography.

Although these patterns of alcohol and other drug (AOD) and pornography use and abuse continued into his young adult life, Richard was able to function at a high level, graduating from high school as valedictorian, spending 4 years in the U.S. Navy, and earning a degree, graduating cum laude, in civil engineering. The degree led to a position as an environmental engineer at a prominent organization in his area. Over the next few years, Richard progressed up the corporate ladder until he reached a point in his late 30s when he was securely established in his profession and his marriage. However, about this same time, he developed physical symptoms of panic attacks, migraines, and a sleeping disorder, and as a result, added tranquilizers, sleeping pills, painkillers, and cocaine to his drugs of choice. Shortly after this, he was divorced and unemployed. For approximately 1 more year, Richard was able to maintain this drug and alcohol use, intermingled with various affairs and severe bouts of depression. At this point, Richard reached a point of desperation. Based on religious involvements from his college years, he sought out help from God and found strength and purpose in moving toward recovery.

After this initial move, Richard relocated to a large city in the Midwest and began a regimen of drug and alcohol counseling and a 12-step group. He attached himself to a religious community where he found support, comfort, a sense of belonging, and an avenue to help others who were experiencing similar AOD struggles. He reported that the withdrawal from cocaine and alcohol took "a month or so" and "wasn't very painful or particularly difficult." He attributed that to the Lord who "truly had mercy on me in that area." He reported that the sexual struggles subsided initially, but the urges to use pornography returned as he increasingly embraced his issues in counseling. He found that he could fight the desires for a while, but then would binge on pornographic material. This pattern continued for a couple of years. He ultimately found help in a church-related program that allowed him to continue in a leadership capacity after his time of training was complete.

Incident

At the time I met Richard, I was counseling in a small clinic, and he was attending a small church-related college nearby. He had been free of his addictions for some time. In fact, he had been free from his dependence on drugs and alcohol for so long that he had come to the conclusion that there was no longer a need for him to avoid people and places where these substances were present.

The particular situation that brought him to my office involved the wedding of one of his close friends. After the wedding reception, several of the friends of the groom decided to go out for drinks and invited him to go. He was fearful at first, but he decided to go based on his long-term sobriety. At the bar where they congregated, one of his friends offered him a beer, which he reasoned would be safe to drink, "since it will be the only one I have." He reported to me that he woke up from a drunken stupor 3 days later in bed with a woman whose name he did not know. He was distressed about "falling off the wagon," and in particular, he felt guilty for not being faithful to God and to the community of faith that had supported him. He was insecure in his sobriety for the first time in a long time and wondered if he had the strength to persevere as an AOD-free person. He was also contemplating withdrawal from college "because I'm a failure in most areas of my life; why will it be any different in school?"

Discussion

Since Richard was convinced that his strength and power had come through God and his community of faith, my approach was to reconnect him to that community so that he could access the characteristics of the community that were valuable and healing to him at this point in his struggle. Initially, although I was relatively sure that his one relapse did not signal a deep-seated dependence, because his weekend had included both alcohol and sex, I felt compelled to do an informal assessment of his dependence. Next, I encouraged him to reestablish his connections with the 12-step group that had been instrumental in his first recovery process. That was the group who had guided him through his recovery through their corporate attachment to God and principles of faith. In that group, I was hoping Richard would experience grace and forgiveness, which would then support his extending of grace and forgiveness to himself. The final step was to reestablish a means for preventing a dive back into sexual addiction. This I did through weekly counseling meeting with me during which we continued the work that he had done prior to coming to my office. This involved exploring behavioral goals for abstaining from pornography and promiscuous sexual behavior, and existential exploration of his meaning and purpose in life as experienced in his relationship and dependence on God.

Questions

1. What other methods might have been used to bring Richard back to stability after his postactive, 3-day relapse into alcohol and sex?
2. From the standpoint of spirituality in counseling, how could a counselor have affirmed Richard's concept of God and God's mercy to him in his recovery in the light of his "falling off the wagon"?
3. How could the religious community to which Richard had connected be more involved in his treatment for both the substance dependence and the sexual addiction? What does the concept of accountability in addictions treatment mean, and how could it have been used to the advantage of the client in this case?

▮Response

Oliver J. Morgan

This case presents a number of elements that are important for an understanding of contemporary substance abuse and dependency counseling.

First, we have a middle-aged man with a substantial *history of multiple drug abuse together with sexual compulsivity*. It is now commonplace to see people in counseling who have moved beyond experimentation with various drugs to patterned use of several drugs. These "drugs of choice" are often used in combination to create a desired biochemical and emotional effect (Khantzian & Schneider, 1985; Milkman & Sunderwirth, 1987). In addition, people struggling with addiction rarely present with a history of only one abused drug or, alternatively, with only abuse of drugs as the issue. Often, there is a corollary process addiction, such as gambling or various kinds of sexual compulsivity, which accompanies the drug abuse (Carnes, 1989; Ciarrocchi, 1987). Consequently, counselors today must attend to several layers and types of compulsivity when dealing with addicted persons.

Second, we are presented with an *incident of relapse and its aftermath*. Relapse is seen so often in work with individuals who struggle with addiction that it can be understood as an integral part of the disorder. Relapse is often the rule rather than the exception, and it has recently been called "the real practical problem" in addiction treatment (Dodes, 2002). Counselors today understand that coping with relapse is part of effective, long-term treatment.

Third, potential *issues of religion, spirituality, and challenges to hope* are deeply embedded in this case. For many people who struggle with abuse and addiction, these issues are often intertwined in their presentation of the problem; they can also, however, be powerful allies in the process of recovery. Today's counselors attend to religious and spiritual issues as potential resources in professional practice.

In this case of a person struggling with multiple addictions, which are now in a postrelapse period, perhaps the most important interventions have already been put into place by the counselor. This professional has worked to reconnect Richard with the community of faith and the 12-step group that have nourished and supported him in his prior recovery. The counselor has also begun weekly sessions to deepen recovery through a mix of behavioral interventions and existential exploration. The counselor's questions at the end of the case address issues of potential other methods of intervention, use of spirituality, and accountability in addictions treatment.

Let me begin my response by stating that 12-step and recovery-oriented treatment are fairly "muscular" forms of healing. They assume and work in a context of support and belonging, and utilize the power of small groups, to stabilize and nourish an initial process of recovery. However, all the while, they have in view a set of tasks—a "recovery project," if you will—that are also necessary for full emotional and spiritual health to take the place of a previous addicted lifestyle. This project includes willingness to change, extensive self-examination, confession to others, acceptance of oneself as is, and alteration of lifestyle, as well as an ongoing combination of prayer/asking for help and service of others. Recovery-oriented treatment of addictions involves both grace *and* work; full spiritual and emotional healing comes as the result of ongoing cooperation with the grace of God. The work of recovery is essential, and it is essentially the catalyst for a "spirituality" of recovery to begin.

In brief, let me respond to the counselor's questions with some clinical suggestions. First, no one successfully changes behavior over the long term without an accompanying change in lifestyle. Just as addiction is a bio-psycho-social and spiritual entity, the thoroughgoing change that is needed must include all those elements as well. This takes *willingness*, a critical motivational and spiritual element (see, e.g., May, 1982, 1988). The counselor in this case would be well served to conduct an assessment for willingness (readiness) to change, using methods of understanding and intervention from both stages-of-change theory (Prochaska, Norcross, & DiClemente, 1994) and motivational interviewing (Miller & Rollnick, 2002). Research has demonstrated the power of these approaches in harnessing the natural change process for ongoing revision of lifestyle.

Second, Richard can benefit from extensive review of his relapse episode, laying out the triggers and cognitive-behavioral cycle that led to relapse (Daley, 1988) and beginning to get a handle on the psychological and emotional factors (e.g., fear, anger, sense of helplessness) that place him at ongoing risk for relapse (Dodes, 2002). Becoming more "mindful"—another spiritual concept—of the factors that contribute to relapse risk, which are often the same challenges that must be handled for ongoing growth, is part of the work of successful recovery. It is also the way to tailor recovery to each person's unique style. This can be done as part of the self-examination, confession, and acceptance that are envisioned by the 12-step process.

This personal review is essential as a way to drain the power from Richard's guilt over his relapse. Scrutinizing the causes and conditions that led to his relapse gives him a different focus and some important spiritual work to do; it can also empower him to feel more confident in his collaboration with "the grace of God." The review I am suggesting should be conducted prayerfully from the perspective of God's (higher power) view of Richard's strengths and growing edges. This may allow him to reclaim a sense of reliance on his "higher power" while setting him an agenda for continued growth in the spiritual life. It may also give him a more realistic sense of self as opposed to the black-and-white thinking in the case presentation.

The truth is that all of us, addicts and those who struggle with ego in other forms, rely on the grace of God and fail from time to time. Richard is no exception. Accepting his fundamental dependence as part of the human condition and his ongoing need for examination and conversion is the catalyst for humility, a virtue that is essential for recovery.

Understanding the unique forms of his dependence and struggle with ego sets an agenda for Richard as a collaborator in his own continued growth. In my experience the issues that underlie one's addiction continue to challenge the person long into recovery; they set the terms for engagement with life over the long term. The case presents Richard's addictive behaviors as deeply reactive to emotional states such as low self-esteem, depression, and panic. There is every reason to believe that these conditions will remain "toxic" for him and potentially risky without a strategy for dealing with them.

The 12-step approaches to healing envision a penetrating search for the underlying roots—psychological, emotional, and characterological—of the conditions that drive addiction. This review is part of the strategy that is needed. The 12 steps speak of "self-will run riot" and "self-centered fear" as the mainsprings of addiction; others speak of issues of "control" (Brown, 1985) or "helplessness" (Dodes, 2002). Richard needs to understand the mechanisms that drive *his* addiction as a way to begin a new recovery, based not on guilt about past failures but rooted in hope for collaborative conversion of lifestyle. Here is a kind of accountability that matters!

This brings me to my third, and final, suggestion. Unfortunately, I do not have a sense from the case presentation about Richard's past spiritual life or lifestyle. I do know that a religious community was helpful in providing support and comfort, and I gather there was also some service to others. However, when we are talking about spirituality as part of the healing task, we are also talking about a *spiritual life and relationship*. High-quality recovery involves a sense of hope and trust in a "Power greater." In my experience this only comes through a long-term relationship with that Power and in the construction of a spiritual life of prayer, connectedness, and service. The counselor, in conjunction with Richard's support groups, sponsor, perhaps also a spiritual adviser, can move Richard toward development of a rich spiritual life as a direct benefit of his recovery from this relapse. Developing some form of regular spiritual practice and/or prayer, in addition to self-examination and confession, would be helpful here. Building a spiritual life around a deepening relationship with one's higher power is critical to the development of spirituality in recovery.

Fostering a regular spiritual practice (e.g., centering prayer, mindfulness meditation, journaling) and working on recovery values and virtues (e.g., humility, honesty, acceptance) are important healing strategies. This work can be nourishing and fruitful for both Richard and his counselor.

These suggestions are offered in the hope that Richard's new recovery will build on what he has learned and will be the catalyst for ongoing development of life to the full.

■References

Brown, S. (1985). *Treating the alcoholic: A developmental model of recovery.* New York: Wiley.

Carnes, P. (1989). *Contrary to love: Helping the sexual addict.* Minneapolis, MN: CompCare.

Ciarrocchi, J. (1987). Severity of impairment in dually addicted gamblers. *Journal of Gambling Behavior, 3,* 16–26.

Daley, D. C. (1988). *Relapse: Conceptual, research and clinical perspectives.* New York: Haworth.

Dodes, L. (2002). *The heart of addiction.* New York: HarperCollins.

Khantzian, E. J., & Schneider, R. J. (1985). Addiction, adaptation, and the "drug-of-choice" phenomenon: Clinical perspectives. In H. B. Milkman & H. J. Shaffer (Eds.), *The addictions: Multidisciplinary perspectives and treatments* (pp. 121–129). Lexington, MA: D.C. Heath.

May, G. G. (1982). *Will and spirit.* San Francisco: Harper & Row.

May, G. G. (1988). *Addiction and grace: Love and spirituality in the healing of addictions.* San Francisco: Harper & Row.

Milkman, H., & Sunderwirth, S. (1987). *Craving for ecstasy: The consciousness and chemistry of escape.* Lexington, MA: D.C. Heath.

Miller, W. R., & Rollnick, S. (2002). *Motivational interviewing: Preparing people for change* (4th ed.). New York: Guilford Press.

Prochaska, J. O., Norcross, J. C., & DiClemente, C. C. (1994). *Changing for good.* New York: Avon.

Critical Incidents in Addictions Counseling

8

Counseling Addicted Gay, Lesbian, Bisexual, and Transgendered Persons

Critical Incident

Luke J. Gilleran

Background

Gays and lesbians and other sexual minorities have alcohol and other drug (AOD) addiction rates estimated at 35%. *Sexual minority* is a term given to those who are gay, lesbian, bisexual, or transgender, and who fall into other categories of sexual and gender status other than what has been considered traditional in the United States. It should be noted that these higher than average addiction rates are not a direct result of *being* a sexual minority. Rather they result from the sexual minority experience—that is, the oppression and discrimination experienced by virtually all sexual minorities each and every day.

Sexual minority status overwhelms all other minority statuses. It has been called the most separating of all minority statuses, in that it most exiles the individual from the rest of society, resulting in numbing isolation. Most minorities rely on family, friends, and church—the most influential and fundamental institutions—for solace and comfort in the face of oppression and discrimination. For sexual minorities, it is these very institutions that reject the person, and by virtue of their importance and influence, necessarily inflict devastating disappointment, loneliness, and despair.

All of these factors lead to interruptions in the identity formation and developmental models into which most populations are assumed to fit. For sexual minorities these models become ineffectual as a predictor of usual identity development. Specifically, during the normal individuation process, which serves in the development of the autonomous adult identity, sexual minorities, because of actual or perceived threats to safety and well-being, avoid many social settings. Consequently, absent is an environment in which the conflicted feelings of teenage years are usually normalized. Because of isolation, sexual minorities often are unable to experiment with facets of identity that ultimately assist in developing a personality that is individual enough to be true, yet conforming enough to be acceptable to the adult population as a whole. In short, identity development of the sexual minority often is stunted, leaving the person without the autonomous adult identity needed to cope with adult situations. As a result, the sexual minority is often chronologically adult, yet developmentally adolescent, resulting in the use of AOD for coping mechanisms in the face of adult stressors (Malyon, 1985).

It should be cautioned not to assume that the presenting gay or lesbian client's difficulties are always a result of their gay experience. Some are able at a very early age to develop the ego strength that protects them from the potential pitfalls facing most gays and lesbians. Therefore, the etiology of every client's difficulties must be carefully discerned. Notwithstanding this point is the fact that a red flag should be seen when a person who is addicted to substances identifies as, or is suspected of, being a sexual minority.

Before revealing the subject of my incident, it is important to disclose that working with gays requires the creation of a gay-affirming atmosphere. Many gay clients will not disclose their sexual orientation because of fear or lack of trust, and it is important to very gently and gradually "sneak up" on the issue and nurture it until the client feels safe to disclose. My goal, therefore, is to communicate my gay-affirming attitudes in nonverbal ways. Throughout my office are books about working with gays, intermingled with other books on counseling. Also present are rainbow flag emblems and other recognitions of gay acceptance and affirmation. I have made sure to use inclusive terminology when referring to relationships and friendships. I have studied any number of "gay glossaries" on the Internet that define many terms relating to issues of gay orientation and culture that are acceptable to the gay community, and I studied the literature on the nature and prevalence of mental health issues facing gays. The importance of communicating a safe and affirming environment cannot be overstated, if one is to draw out a client's gay sexual identity.

Incident

Dwayne is a 27-year-old gay man presenting with drug dependence and a history of relapse. His employer referred him to treatment after the results of a random urine toxicology screen indicated drug use. Dwayne has an undergraduate degree in history, is single, and has no co-occurring medical conditions. This is his first experience in addiction treatment. During our first meeting, after glancing around my office and commenting on the indications of my gay-affirming attitude, Dwayne disclosed his sexual orientation.

In completing the bio-psycho-social intake with Dwayne, it was important to gather a history of substance use, including the specific drugs, age of first use of each, the amount used during peak usage times, the frequency of use, the most recent amounts of usage, and the last time he used each substance. Not only is this integral to applying diagnostic criteria of the *Diagnostic and Statistical Manual of Mental Disorders* (4th ed., Text Revision [*DSM-IV-TR*]; American Psychiatric Association, 2000), also it indicates whether or not he will need a formal detoxification program as he attempts to achieve abstinence. This latter point is extremely important, as detoxification can present myriad accompanying health threats and in extreme cases can be fatal. Dwayne's drug of choice was crack cocaine, which does not promote physical tolerance, and therefore needed no inpatient detoxification. Additionally, patterns of usage may be compared to the timeline of events in Dwayne's life to illustrate potential links between circumstances and increased substance use.

In substance abuse treatment, it is important to deal with the condition that poses the more immediate threat to the client. In Dwayne's case, as in the case of many addicted clients, the first goal is the attainment of abstinence from the addiction that threatens his employment, health, and potentially his life. No meaningful work can be done on any co-occurring mental disorder or issues while the client is under the influence of AOD. Moreover, achieving abstinence from AOD often answers the question of whether the AOD has caused the co-occurring condition or whether the AOD was used as a mechanism of coping with the co-occurring condition. Full psychological evaluation should not be undertaken before the client has 2 weeks to 1 month of complete abstinence from AOD. Consequently, we began to focus on Dwayne's recovery from AOD addiction.

Because Dwayne had no prior treatment for addiction, we started with basic education. The disease concept of addiction was discussed, as was the concept of 12-step recovery. After 3 weeks of complete abstinence from all AOD, and the establishment of a baseline recovery program to which Dwayne had committed, we began to look at the issues that may form the basis for his addictive behavior. Suspecting the gay experience as a fundamental contributor to the need for coping behavior, I began to ask Dwayne about his sexual orientation.

It has been written that the number one predictor of mental health or illness in gays is the degree to which internalized homophobia is present (Gonsiorek, 1988). Internalized homophobia is a phenomenon whereby gays assimilate some or all of the negative messages to which they have been exposed over the course of their lives thus far. The constant bombardment by these messages makes it nearly impossible to avoid some level of internalized homophobia that ranges from subtle dissatisfaction with the trials of being gay to out-and-out self-loathing. I asked Dwayne to disclose to whom he was "out" and to whom he chose to hide his sexual orientation. Much can be discerned about the presence of internalized homophobia from the rationale behind the answers to these questions. Although there are instruments designed to measure internalized homophobia, I believe the questions that make them up are so broad and general, a low score can be obtained that fails to uncover the subtle forms. At the beginning of each subsequent session, the status of Dwayne's recovery from addiction is the first focus. Only after it is clear that he has remained abstinent in the prior week and is doing the things necessary to remain so do I segue to the topic of sexual orientation.

Dwayne disclosed that he was out to his siblings but not his parents. He felt they would be devastated by the disclosure. Additionally, Dwayne is closeted at his place of employment. He stated he has mostly straight friends because he wishes to be in the mainstream and values his gay status as just a small part of who he is. It became clear to me from our discussions that Dwayne suffered from a significant level of internalized homophobia. Denying himself the option of being openly gay in most aspects of his life and his desire to remain in the mainstream and not experience gay associations and culture indicate that on some level he believes there is something undesirable or simply wrong with being gay. In essence, Dwayne was an outsider to both the straight and gay communities. Thus, I devoted the majority of our session time to discussing sexual orientation. This was done in an effort to challenge the cognitive distortions emanating from his internalized homophobia. In addition, I encouraged Dwayne to gradually connect with the gay community and culture. Obviously, I needed to provide resources through which he could begin to connect, without threatening his fragile recovery. Initially, I gave him the addresses of several gay 12-step meetings in his area so he could begin to find a gay social network that included other gays in recovery from addiction. In doing so, the goals were to expose Dwayne to healthy gay modeling, to foster a sense of belonging, and to receive affirmation to counter the negative messages he has received day after day.

Discussion

After several months of sessions, Dwayne remained abstinent and began to connect to the gay community. He began to see his gayness not as something to be endured, but as a special gift that allowed him to be an accepted member of a unique group. As appropriate, Dwayne began to come out to more people and finally came out to his parents, who, as is often the case, stated they suspected his gayness but waited for him to broach the subject. In our subsequent discussions about coming out and about the current politics of gay marriage and civil unions, Dwayne began to assume the "us against them" position that indicates his identification with gays as a minority group. And Dwayne was elected chairperson of his gay 12-step group.

Questions

1. In what other ways should counselors prepare themselves to work with gay clients?
2. How might you continue to safely foster Dwayne's immersion in the gay community while simultaneously encouraging him to avoid the part of gay culture that emphasizes drug and alcohol use?
3. What other structured therapeutic environments do you believe would help Dwayne overcome his internalized homophobia and feel a sense of belonging in both the gay and straight communities?

Critical Incidents in Addictions Counseling

■Response

Stuart F. Chen-Hayes

The addictions counselor's strengths here include the importance of focusing on how the addiction occurred in the context of heterosexism, both internalized and externalized. The counselor focuses appropriately on abstinence for the client through the use of 12-step groups and cognitive-behavioral interventions and assists the client in discussing fears and concerns about living life affirmatively as a gay man.

In addition to these suggested interventions and specific target issues, a broader focus, inclusive of inherent cultural and family issues, is needed. For example, eliminate the phrase *sexual minority*, as this term is one that is accurate in terms of government politics (e.g., the Democrats are in the minority in the Senate) but not for members of oppressed groups based on nondominant cultural identities. In addition, the term *minority* when applied to people of color is simply inaccurate (87% of the world's population are people of color). When applied to lesbian, bisexual, gay, transgendered, and queer (LBGTQ) persons, the term *minority* is often interpreted incorrectly as "less than" rather than less in terms of sheer numbers of individuals self-describing with this particular label.

The author states that sexual orientation status is the most oppressed status among identified oppressed groups, and yet there is no empirical evidence in support of this assertion. Most LBGTQ people of color would argue that they are equally oppressed by racism and heterosexism, and lesbians of color would argue that sexism adds to create a triple set of oppressions in their lives. With physical appearance a major determinant of social status in gay communities, issues of beautyism and ableism are also key for many gay men. Therefore, the counseling process with this particular client might be further enhanced by considering the intersections of multiple cultural identities in the client's life (Robinson, 2005) and how to effectively advocate for addressing multiple oppressions in LBGTQ counseling (Chen-Hayes, 2003).

Finally, the author may want to reconsider the assumption that individuation in this particular case can be viewed as "normal," as this is not supported within families of color with a traditional worldview and strong levels of pride in their ethnic/racial identity development (Sue & Sue, 2003). For many persons of color, the traditional identity development process focuses on a collective identity (Sue & Sue, 2003); an individual-based model of development is seen as a White or European worldview that may even be dismissed as "selling out." Ultimately, Dwayne might benefit from a clearer focus and direct application of both his and his counselor's multiple cultural identities in the counseling process.

Ironically, neither the client's nor the counselor's ethnic and racial identities are discussed. In an effort to ensure cultural competence, as well as success with this client, ethnic/racial identity information seems essential. If, for example, the client is an African American (likely with a mixture of African, Native American, and European ethnicities), as are the majority of urban crack cocaine users in the United States, his racial and ethnic identities need to be acknowledged and affirmed. In the same way the counselor acknowledged and worked with Dwayne's gay identity, his other affiliations need to be considered within the counseling process. This is essential in terms of the psychological ramifications in this case, but the more tangible consequences of getting caught, as well as issues of jail time distributed and served, vary according to racial identity. For example, penalties for possession of crack cocaine by Blacks are much worse than for use and possession of powder cocaine, which has been used in the United States primarily by White cocaine users. In addition, individuals of color tend to serve longer jail terms and are associated with significantly higher conviction rates than White offenders. African Americans have not had high rates of success in counseling as a whole, including addictions work, because of poor cultural awareness, knowledge, and skills with clients of color on the part of counselors, who often lack what Sue and Sue (2003) referred to as trust and credibility in working with Black clients.

I would also conduct a complete psychosocial history. I would gather information relevant to Dwayne's family background and significant other(s) or dating history. In addition, I would assess the status of coexisting addictions, as well as addictions present within other family members currently and in past generations. I would assess Dwayne's history in terms of how his disease has progressed to his current use patterns with crack cocaine and what his alcohol and other drug history has been with other substances. Ironically, even in Black gay communities, crack cocaine is not as widespread as the use of alcohol, marijuana, or designer club drugs such as ecstasy and crystal meth. In many gay party scenes with men of various racial identities, however, powder cocaine is more likely to be available. In light of the current rates of HIV/AIDS for men (and women) of African descent around the world, I would also want to assess current behavioral practices related to safer sex. It may then be important to discuss the evidence suggestive of the significant relationship between use of drugs before or during sex and the increased likelihood of engaging in unsafe sexual practices that can lead to HIV/AIDS and other sexually transmitted infections.

The spiritual component of the recovery process has been well documented and highly supported. Twelve-step programs utilize the concept of a higher power as absolutely central to the recovery process. In this case, the counselor refers to "church" in his work with Dwayne. It may be more beneficial to use a term such as "place of worship" to ensure an inclusive tone and pattern within the counseling process. Many gay men, including Black men, have grown up with "church" defining gay as bad or sinful, and this association often encourages feelings of shame. Ultimately, Dwayne must struggle with the notion of finding meaning. This particular piece of his journey might be better facilitated through challenging oppressions such as racism and heterosexism and constructing a spiritual framework that can facilitate rather than delay healing. In addition, it may be beneficial for Dwayne to learn more about the rich history of powerful men of African descent. Exploring the work of Bayard Rustin in the civil rights movement or the poetry of Essex Hemphill or the prose of James Baldwin would all be possibilities for a client to affirm his gay and Black identities through the words and stories of other gay African Americans. There also needs to be more of a focus on the counselor's (presumably White) ethnic/racial identity development and worldview and how the counselor's own skills in this area could be critical for the success or failure of the counseling with a client of color.

Ultimately, the counselor needs to assist Dwayne in the development of skills and resources that he can use to advocate on his own behalf. Dwayne will need to establish practices and behaviors that allow for clean and sober spaces for socializing and developing a support network. This might include Internet chat rooms, as well as alcohol- and drug-free dances and coffeehouses, for dating and meeting up with friends or dates. It would be critical for Dwayne to develop a group of gay friends to socialize with who do not drink and use drugs to support his recovery. In addition, it would seem essential to assist Dwayne in identifying potential triggers that may encourage relapse, along with the development of a plan to counteract triggers when they do present. This could be done within the context of both discussion and role-playing in an effort to solidify, through practice, a set of responses that might facilitate healthy responses to triggers.

Structured healing environments that might benefit Dwayne in his recovery could include group counseling with other men of color who are clean and sober, as well as support groups at a local LBGTQ Center or online, if such a facility is not available. Use of narrative counseling (White & Epston, 1991) could be especially useful in helping Dwayne find stories to which he might easily relate, narratives in which nondominant heroes experience success in life. Specifically, stories might encourage Dwayne to strengthen his gay identity, his Black identity, and challenge the oppressive heterosexist discourses that may have led to his drug dependence and could prove enormously beneficial. Finally, assisting Dwayne in considering developing a clean and sober gay "family of choice" would also be an effective strategy.

■References

American Psychiatric Association. (2000). *Diagnostic and statistical manual of mental disorders* (4th ed., Text Revision). Washington, DC: Author.

Chen-Hayes, S. F. (2003). Challenging multiple oppressions with GLBT clients. In J. S. Whitman & C. J. Boyd (Eds.), *The therapist's notebook for lesbian, gay, and bisexual clients: Homework, handouts, and activities for use in psychotherapy* (pp. 174–178). Binghamton, NY: Haworth Clinical Practice Press.

Gonsiorek, J. (1988). Mental health issues of gay and lesbian adolescents. *Journal of Adolescent Health Care, 9,* 114–122.

Malyon, A. (1985). *Psychotherapeutic implications of internalized homophobia in gay men: A guide to psychotherapy with gay and lesbian clients.* New York: Harrington Park Press.

Robinson, T. L. (2005). *The convergence of race, ethnicity, and gender: Multiple identities in counseling.* Boston: Pearson Merrill Prentice Hall.

Sue, D. W., & Sue, D. (2003). *Counseling the culturally diverse: Theory and practice* (4th ed.). New York: Wiley.

White, M., & Epston, D. (1991). *Narrative means to therapeutic ends.* New York: Norton.

Critical Incidents in Addictions Counseling

9

Addictions Counseling
With African Americans

■Critical Incident

Shawn L. Spurgeon

Background

James was a 27-year-old African American male who lived with his 25-year-old wife, Karen; their two children, 6-year-old James Jr. and 3-year-old Kali; and James's mother, Barbara. James had two younger sisters who lived far away from the family unit. James's sisters believed that they would never amount to anything if they remained in the neighborhood. They returned only for special occasions (holidays, birthday celebrations, etc.). James's father died from a cocaine overdose when James was 10, and his two uncles took on the responsibility of providing a positive male role model for him. James was very athletic in school and participated in numerous sports before graduating from high school and earning an athletic scholarship to play basketball at a Division III school. Karen and James met in college during his junior year and married after James graduated from college with a degree in physical education. Karen left college after the birth of James Jr. during her sophomore year and never returned to finish.

James spent most of his life around his family and extended family and developed deep and meaningful relationships in the community. James wanted to teach in the public school system but could not pass the PRAXIS examination and had to take a job as an assistant manager for the local grocery store. Karen was unable to find adequate work and stayed home to care for the children. Eventually, James began to participate in an "underground economy" (gambling, betting, etc.) to meet the family's economic needs.

During our initial clinical interview, James admitted that he and Karen often argued about finances and raising the children. James was experiencing significant stress in the following areas: (a) role identity, (b) financial security, (c) perceived familial discord, and (d) asking for and accepting help. James stated that he did not need to attend counseling and was only participating as a part of his agreement with the district attorney and the Department of Social Services. In a separate interview, Karen stated that James believed he was not successful enough and that he had let his family down. Karen admitted that James had pushed her several times during arguments but that he was very gentle with the children.

Incident

James was referred for counseling by the district attorney after his fifth DWI and a child endangerment charge. While under the influence, he ran into his neighbor's telephone pole while his son was riding with him. James's license was suspended for 1 year, and the children were placed with a relative by the Department of Social Services. As a part of his treatment, he was given probation and community service for restitution of damages and ordered to attend counseling by the district attorney and the Department of Social Services. James initially refused the deal but agreed after encouragement from his extended family members and friends.

During our first counseling session James provided me with a snapshot of his life. James grew up in a "rough" neighborhood and stated that he had to fight everyday to protect himself until people realized his athletic talent and strength and "left him alone." He admitted to selling drugs "once or twice" when he was 11 but stated that he never used them. However, James did disclose that he started drinking at the age of 10 to help him deal with the loss of his father. He stated that alcohol was a normal part of his life and that his extended family never discouraged him from drinking. James was most oppositional when he drank heavily and usually argued with Karen when he was intoxicated.

James was hesitant to talk about his family of origin but eventually identified his role as the caretaker of the family. He had worked in high school to help his mother with the bills and spent his summers working full time so that his sisters would have new clothes to wear to school. He was adamant about attending college because he felt that he needed to set the example for his sisters to follow. James was the first one in his family to attend and to graduate from college and stated that he often felt the pressure of "being the first." Alcohol helped him deal more effectively with the situation by providing him with an outlet for the pressure and frustration he felt.

During this initial counseling session, several things emerged that seemed to be important. First, James viewed himself as the caretaker of the family. The success or failure of the family and extended family units clearly rested on his shoulders. Second, James used alcohol to self-medicate and numb the stress related to the realities of his existence. Though James had achieved some things in his life, he saw his existence as marginal and used alcohol to help him deal with his feelings of failure. Third, James was very loyal to his family. Although he admitted to his participation in activities that had led to his current troubles, he openly expressed that he would "do it again," even though the potential for significant jail time existed. Finally, James clearly had not dealt with his father's death. Though his life changed dramatically after his father's death, James did not talk much about his father during our initial session.

The assessment and initial session served as a baseline for how I would work with James and his situation. James arrived 10 minutes late to the next session and immediately apologized for his tardiness. I thanked James for being willing to continue to discuss his concerns with me, and he stated that he is simply trying to fulfill his obligation to the Department of Social Services so that he can get his son back. I summarized our initial session and asked if he would be willing to talk more about his father; he respectfully declined. I then facilitated a discussion with him about what he wanted to get out of this process. His response was, "Whatever they think I need," and I encouraged him to think about what he would need from this process. He stated, "I need for people to leave me alone and let me live my life. That's something you will not be able to give me."

I encouraged James to complete a cost-benefit analysis with me regarding his current mentality related to his situation. We talked about the benefits of continued nonparticipation and the costs of nonparticipation. Also, we talked about the benefits of participation and the costs of participation. James reluctantly agreed that his best approach would be to cooperate with the recommendations made by the Department of Social Services and the district attorney.

I encouraged James to take a step back and look at his situation by using a life script technique. I allowed James to create a mental timeline of the significant events in his life and to discuss those events at whatever level he felt comfortable. I made connections by pointing out the similarities between his life and my own; he seemed to relax more and spoke more freely about his existence. James stated that he always felt an intense pressure since his father passed away and provided concrete examples using the life script approach. He stated that he often felt unheard by society and by his family and that he needed to stay focused and "keep everybody else up." He agreed that his main support was alcohol and that he used it to deal with the different pressures and responsibilities that were placed on him by his situation. "When I'm drinking, I'm in a different world."

James stated that he enjoyed this session because he felt comfortable talking about issues with me and he did not hear "the district attorney's voice" in his head. He stated that he wanted to continue to see me and that eventually he would be willing to talk in more detail about his interpersonal struggles. I encouraged James to consider the fact that this process can be very beneficial and can be an effective way to deal with his interpersonal struggles. James agreed that the benefits of counseling would be much greater than spending time in jail. He agreed to sign release forms for the Department of Social Services and district attorney, who were assigned to evaluate his progress after 6 months.

Discussion

James portrayed an active and sometimes difficult life that came to a point with this accident. As a result, other people (Department of Social Services, courts) were forced to make decisions about his life that he normally reserved for himself. James was very adamant about keeping his business to himself and expressed no desire to actively participate in counseling. However, after a cost-benefit analysis was completed during the second session, James agreed that the most effective way to resolve his situation was to comply with the state's recommendations.

Questions

1. Given the situation, I diagnosed James with alcohol dependence and depression. Given his hesitancy to participate in the counseling process, can you think of any other interventions that you may have used instead of or in conjunction with the life script analysis?
2. Given the nature of addictions and based on the available literature related to addictions with African American males, how effective would other forms of counseling be in this situation (group, couples, family)? Would any of these be more effective than individual counseling?
3. There is a clear mistrust of the justice system among African American males. Any suggestions on how to ensure a client such as this one that he is doing counseling with me and that I am different from the person who has mandated treatment?
4. How important are the cultural issues related to alcohol use among African American males in this situation, and how do I integrate these issues into treatment with James?

Response

Michael Arthur

In the case presented, the counselor has done a thorough job of conceptualizing the issues that the client has presented. Furthermore, the counselor has been able to establish a good relationship with a client who initially was not interested in pursing counseling. This is especially remarkable given the high level of resistance present at the start of the counseling process. In contrast to when they first met, the client is now willingly discussing his life and has signed forms that will allow the counselor to inform both the Department of Social Services and the attorney general's office of his progress.

Because building trust and establishing a therapeutic relationship is so crucial to progress, the counselor seeks out approaches and strategies that might enhance the achievement of this goal. The counselor poses several questions that are rooted in the issues of building trust and establishing the therapeutic relationship. It seems that the counselor is seeking an answer to the following question: How is it possible for a client forced to enter counseling, by a justice system he mistrusts, not to view the counselor as part of the establishment he considers to be the core of the problems he faces? In this particular case, the counselor is, in fact, a part of this system. This dialectic both challenges and provides opportunities that can enrich the counseling process and help the client move beyond the issues that are affecting his life.

It important that the counselor come to terms with the implicit contradictions inherent in this point, which include significantly conceding that the client's stance is not completely irrational. Within the set of circumstances that are described in this case, the counselor is part of a set of institutional relationships that are aimed at holding the client accountable for his behaviors, demanding changes in behavior, or facing, alternatively, the consequences for failing to do so. In other words, the counselor is initially perceived by the client to be a part of the problem and not part of any healthy alternative solutions.

Many would argue that an African American male is appropriately skeptical about institutions that have anything to do with law enforcement because of the institutional racism that is part of the legacy of American society. Because the counselor works for one of these institutions, he is placed in a position that implies he cannot be trusted. The counselor has to find a way to earn the trust of his client and maintain this trust until the process is ended. Even if the counselor is African American, he will not secure instant credibility with this client. And although the client has a college degree, he may see the African American counselor—though educated like the client—as one who is working for the system and against the client. This, of course, is also influenced by and dependent on where the client is in his own racial identity development. Lee (1999) might describe a client such as this to be in the dissonance phase, because he is experiencing psychological conflict as he comes to realize the impact of culture on his own life. A counselor from a similar or same ethnic group, or one who is knowledgeable about the client's culture would, of course, be very helpful at this stage.

The counselor noted that the client displays "hesitancy to participate" in the counseling process because of "the mistrust of the justice system." This hesitancy, from the client's perspective, can be interpreted as seeing the counselor as guilty and culpable just by being a counselor at the Department of Social Services, a form of guilt by association, in terms of the way the client views the counselor. However, I cannot agree that this resistance faced by the counselor at the start of the process is untoward; rather it is to be expected. I view their relationship as reflecting the cultural context in which they both exist. The counselor needs to use his training in culturally sensitive ways and go about the process of bridging the gaps between himself and the client.

Once viewed from this perspective, the counselor is psychologically liberated to go about establishing the relationship without being unduly burdened by the notion that the client is resistant. This turns the process from one of wondering if the relationship can be established to exploring how it is being established. This in turn puts responsibility on the shoulders of the counselor, as a trained mental health professional, to do what is expected—to see the client as fully human, with flaws and strengths, and a humanity that must be engaged despite how it is initially presented in counseling by the client.

This brings us to the question of exactly what kind of intervention works to help establish the relationship. What are the kinds of statements that the counselor could make that would build trust and establish the relationship? From my experience in working with men who are referred to counseling because they are in trouble with the law, the counselor should always establish a nonjudgmental form of interacting with the clients, one that is clearly very respectful of the client. The tenets of the Rogerian model should be adhered to in the initial and other stages of the counseling process.

In this model, valuing the client means that counselor accepts their particular circumstances and then seeks to communicate to the client the honest reality of their relationship. Because there is no doubt that the counselor works for the establishment, the therapist should communicate this reality and not allow it to further occupy the therapeutic space. Furthermore, the counselor should tell the client that he, the counselor, recognizes the inequality in the relationship and the client can reasonably infer the counselor has significant power over him and that this could make it difficult for the client to desire to put trust in the counselor. The counselor should also state that the nature of his job is to report the progress of the client back to the relevant authorities and that this will happen with or without the client's cooperation. The counselor should also acknowledge that the legal system and other institutions have a history of being unfair to African Americans and that an African American male who comes into contact with the justice system has every reason to doubt that it would be helpful to him. Finally, the counselor might admit that he does not know the client's unique circumstances and cannot pretend that he knows the client's life, that seeking help is not always easy, and that the client may consequently feel a sense of weakness in getting help. However, at the point this counselor also needs to ask the permission of the client to intervene in his life and seek to engage the client's help in resolving the issues he is confronting. This puts some power back into the hands of the client without compromising the integrity of either the client or the counselor. It also deals with the issue of shame in a humane and sensitive way.

While the counselor is doing all this, he must not fear making a mistake but be open to the possibility that this could happen. If or when it does occur, he must be honest in dealing with it as an error and not as a flaw. Finally, the counselor must be aware of his own stereotypes, not impose them on the client, and remain aware of how his own cultural heritage informs the current relationship.

This kind of active, respectful stance allows for the coexistence of the differences between the client and the counselor. They are, in fact, brought fully into the open. It suggests the counselor concedes that he may be different from the client and he is not pretending to be the same as the client. Counselors who cannot handle differences in this way only insult their clients and inhibit the counseling relationship.

The issue of the interventions then becomes of greater importance once the client is willing to trust the therapist. However, a more active role on the part of the counselor may be indicated at this juncture in the relationship. Lee (1999) suggested that African American clients may not respond well to passive styles of therapeutic intervention and that more active interventions like

Critical Incidents in Addictions Counseling

cognitive-behavioral approaches provide a better cultural fit for the amelioration of mental health issues. With this in mind, it is important to find therapeutic interventions that challenge the client's irrational beliefs. Rational emotive behavioral therapy is, in my view, an example of an approach that does this well. By challenging the client to alter his beliefs in the face of unchanging life events, the therapist is introducing a set of techniques that relate to the present circumstances in the client's life and have real practical application. This learning may give the client the confidence to apply this approach in the more public setting required for group and family therapy.

A rational emotive approach may also help the client deal with the issues of shame he feels in not being able to provide for his family financially. It may also help him reevaluate the core beliefs that inform his sense of being responsible for both his own family and his extended family. Finally, it may assist the client in challenging the beliefs that prevent him from talking about the death of his father.

According to Lee (1999), group counseling is effective with African Americans. Once the client has acquired the skills to challenge his own irrational thinking, graduating to group work can also be a powerful tool. In a men's group, the other clients might enhance the process of identity development for this client. The advantage of this group approach is that other men typically have the credibility, confirm the reality of, and then challenge notions that are problematic. Furthermore, a male group can introduce the notion of joint equal partnership in marriage, facilitating the ability of the wife to use her own talents.

Family therapy might also be considered as another modality that can facilitate change and encourage growth. The culturally skilled counselor would look to understand how this client defines what he means by family. There is ample evidence to support the notion that for African Americans family is not just blood relatives but can include others who have been there historically to provide help (Lee, 1999). Couples therapy may provide an avenue to explore what it means to this client to be a husband.

The role of alcohol as a drug of choice for James is of interest to me. I believe that it is important to note that James's dad died from a cocaine overdose. Could it be that because his dad died from a cocaine overdose James has too many negative associations with this drug? Cocaine may not be preferred by James because of what it represents—the death of his father. What does it mean that he has chosen alcohol? Also, it is worth asking both in the group and individual setting about some of the dominant memories James has of his father and if any of these entail drug abuse.

If the counselor is convinced that cultural messages around alcohol use need to be incorporated in treatment, then this should be explored. But first it requires that that the counselor ask about the symbolic nature of alcohol in the Black community. Historically, James had positive relationships in the community and may care about his community and what alcohol represents. Alcohol, like other drugs, some that James used to sell, are meaning-making symbols. In the case of alcohol, it is a means of facilitating pain and is a coping mechanism for Blacks in poverty. It may be that given James's own relationship with the drug, and how it has impeded his own growth, he is willing to look at the political implications of having drugs in his community.

James may be willing to engage and ask questions like, Why is it that liquor stores show up in communities where people are so economically disenfranchised? Why is it that alcohol becomes one of so few options for those living in rough neighborhoods? Who is benefiting from the use of this sort of drug by Blacks? How is it alcohol is legal even though it is a leading cause of death in the United States? These questions have significant political undertones and implications. If James is interested, some social change issues could be incorporated into his own personal change issues. However, I would caution that James needs to be able to take care of himself first before he can find other outlets for his anger. In addition, issues such as these could be assessed by understanding where James is in terms of his own racial identity development.

I see James as a young man who could benefit from working closely with a counselor individually, in family therapy, and in couples therapy. I also see James as person who could benefit from group therapy. His case is one where improvement is possible.

■Reference

Lee, W. M. L. (1999). *An introduction to multicultural counseling.* Philadelphia: Accelerated Development.

Critical Incidents in Addictions Counseling

10
Latinos and Addictions Counseling

■Critical Incident

Nicole J. Pizzini

Background

Twenty-two-year-old Yarrette is a first-generation born Puerto Rican American. She currently lives with her husband, Manuel, of 2 years, in an apartment just down the street from her parents. Yarrette is currently in her 3rd month of her first pregnancy. She and her husband are very excited about the pending birth of her baby. Yarette was born to parents who came to the United States 5 years before she was born. Her father worked in a factory, and her mother stayed at home to raise the children, two girls and a son. Yarette is the oldest child in her family. There were many expectations for her, the foremost being that she would follow the traditional ways by being a good wife and good mother. As she grew up, Yarette did well in school, getting mostly A's and a couple of B's. She did not participate in extracurricular activities as she had to come home to help out her mom with the other kids. Yarette always wanted to participate in other school activities, but she knew she could not and never asked to participate. Yarette was very close to her mother, but not so much with her father. Her father liked to drink heavily after he came home from long hours at work. Her father expected her to help her mother by taking care of him and the other children. Her father was a violent man when he drank as he often hit his wife and son. These occurrences happened only while he was drinking. When he was not drinking he was a happy, funny man. Yarette's friends did not like to come to their house because of the way her father acted when he consumed alcohol. Yarette's friends did not drink or use drugs.

After graduation, Yarette lived at home and continued to help out her mother. She started going to the local bars where she first experienced alcohol. Yarette found that drinking made her more relaxed and comfortable around her friends and strangers she would meet in the bar. Soon Yarrette was drinking a couple times a week to the point of intoxication. She returned home one night after drinking to find her father waiting for her. He was extremely angry and threatened to kick her out of the house if she ever came home that way again. This did not deter Yarette from drinking; she just started to hide her drinking from her parents.

As she was still living at home, it was expected that she attend church with the family. This is where she met her current husband shortly after she graduated high school. Manuel was born in Puerto Rico and is a couple of years older than Yarette. He came to the United States to complete his college education and did not plan to return to Puerto Rico for a few years. They courted for about 1 year and then were married at their church. Their marriage has been full of ups and downs due to issues surrounding role expectations and Yarette's desire for independence. Yarette has also been hiding her alcohol use from her husband and her family.

Incident

A few months ago, an ER doctor and hospital social worker referred Yarette to counseling following an admission to the hospital related to a car accident. Yarette was home awaiting the arrival of her husband while she was drinking alcohol. Her nightly routine was to drink three rum and cokes before her husband returned from his second shift job. This evening she was called on by her mother to go to the store to buy some groceries. Yarette reluctantly agreed but proceeded to drive her car to the store. On her way there she had a blackout and hit a telephone pole. An ambulance was called and she was taken to the hospital. At the hospital it was discovered she had consumed alcohol as her blood alcohol level was .06, and it was also discovered she was pregnant. Her mother started to worry when she did not show up within an hour. Her mother called Manuel at his work to see if he knew anything. He stated he thought his wife was at home. They became concerned and called the police. Upon investigating, it was discovered Yarette was at the local hospital. Manuel and Yarette's mother went to the hospital to find Yarette alert and without major injury. Manuel and Yarette were informed she was pregnant and that her alcohol use could have an impact on her unborn child.

Discussion

Because of the recent hospitalization and referral to treatment, Manuel and Yarette started attending counseling sessions. Manuel was extremely angry that she could have put their baby in danger and that she was consuming alcohol. Yarette was torn between her desire to have some independence and her apparent "failure" as a mother. She denied issues with alcohol use, even though an assessment indicated she was a heavy drinker. Specific concerns focus on Yarette and her alcohol consumption and potential risks to the baby should Yarette continue drinking. Other concerns relate to role conflicts Yarette is experiencing.

Questions

1. Given the nature of the circumstances, what type of intervention related to alcohol issues would you consider?

2. Knowing that family support is extremely important, how would you involve Yarette's family members in the counseling sessions?
3. There appears to be conflict around Yarette's belief concerning her roles in her relationship with her husband. How might you explore these beliefs without imparting your own values of family, independence, autonomy, and gender norms?

■Response

Albert A. Valadez

Yarette is facing acculturation issues related to being a first-generation American. American culture does not have as well-defined gender role expectations as compared with many Latino cultures. Therefore, many Latina first-generation clients experience cultural conflicts between traditional family values and those associated with being an American woman. The tension and pressure associated with the conflict of expectations can result in frustration, confusion about cultural identity, and acculturation stress, which can lead to maladaptive coping such as excessive alcohol and other drug use.

With the conflict of expectations in mind, there are important cultural concepts that one might consider when constructing a treatment plan with Manuel and Yarette. The first one, *personalismo*, has implications for the counseling relationship. *Personalismo* emphasizes the importance of personal contact. It is believed each individual's characteristics or *personalismo* become exhibited in the context of the human relationships. A detached counseling relationship could result in precipitous termination. In an attempt to make personal contact, Latino clients might be inclined to bring food to session or to ask the counselor personal questions about his or her family. The culturally competent counselor could use self-disclosure to exhibit his or her personal characteristic to help join with the couple or family to form a trusting relationship.

In response to Question 1 regarding types of interventions, I would initially use a directive approach. When loss or impairment of life is possible, it is important to accurately assess the level of physical dependency on alcohol. Enduring withdrawal symptoms during the early stages of pregnancy can have negative consequences on the fetus. If it is determined that Yarette is physically dependent, then consultation with a medical expert is necessary and inpatient treatment must be put on the table as a possibility. If physical dependency is not indicated, then the drinking will simply have to cease. The counselor should seek an agreement, for the safety of the unborn child, to get rid of any alcohol in the house.

A second important concept that is associated with Puerto Rican and other Latino cultures is *marianismo*. *Marianismo* emphasizes that a woman's path to complete self-fulfillment is found in motherhood. Self-sacrifices for the children, husband, and household are strong expectations. Harming a child, especially as a result of self-indulgence, is frowned on. Therefore, it is very likely that Yarette is experiencing a great deal of shame because her drinking, although unintentional, could have possibly harmed her baby. Although Yarette is struggling with issues regarding independence, it does not necessarily mean that she has rejected values associated with *marianismo*. It would be beneficial to provide Yarette the opportunity to express her feelings of shame and regret. In addition, an action-oriented approach focused on giving her every opportunity to have a healthy pregnancy should be explored.

One action-oriented approach is to examine the historical environmental factors that existed when she did not drink. Using a solution-focused approach helps to identify these factors and is the first step to creating a healthier lifestyle. For example, when Yarette was in school she never drank or did drugs. Members of her social network also abstained. Yarette seemed to value performing well in school, and it is possible to infer that her high academic performance built her esteem. Perhaps, rather than waiting for her husband to come home from work she could be enrolled in preparenting classes that are often sponsored by local hospitals. This intervention would serve two purposes: (a) occupy time she would otherwise use to drink and (b) give Yarette a sense of pride knowing she is doing what she can to help her baby be healthy.

A third cultural concept that addresses male role expectations in a familial or interpersonal context is *machismo*. *Machismo* is often associated with male dominance and sexual aggression over women. However, these largely perceived negative descriptors of "being macho" does not include other traditionally held beliefs of what it means to be a man. First and foremost, being the protector of one's family is of utmost importance. Being the financial provider, defending the family's honor, and exhibiting *respeto* or respect toward others, especially authority figures, are important components as well. While Manuel's anger is certainly justified and should be validated, the counselor might consider how to enlist Manuel as a facilitator for Yarette to have a healthy pregnancy. As the provider and proctor of his future family, he could benefit from becoming aware that his anger and blaming likely only create more stress for Yarette, thus potentially harming the baby.

A fourth cultural concept that addresses Question 2 involves *familismo,* or the emphasis on family unity and the maintenance of extended family relationships. In large part, members of traditional Puerto Rican families initially look to immediate and extended family, neighbors, and religious figures to help solve life problems. Seeking out a counselor for help is generally not the first option for many Latinos. This interdependency among family and community members is a source of great strength and can be utilized by the counselor in working with Yarette and Manuel.

For example, I would dialogue with Yarette regarding the identification of supportive members of her social and familial network: family members or friends she trusts and feels will not judge her negatively. These individuals could be integrated in the counseling session on an as-needed basis. I would facilitate an honest dialogue between Yarette and selected members of her network as to how they could assist in helping her abstain from alcohol.

Addressing concerns expressed in Question 3 is going to require commitment from both Yarette and Manuel to closely examine their relationship. Given that Manuel is new to the United States, there is a high likelihood that his level of acculturation is low, and his traditional expectations related to a woman's self-sacrifice for husband and children reflect his experiences and upbringing in Puerto Rico. Therefore, there is likely to be strife in the marriage if the exploration of Yarette's personal interests takes time away from caring for the home and family. Unfortunately, the distress associated with exploring one's own interests might come from some members of Yarette's family, especially females who are generally charged with preserving cultural customs and traditions.

The marriage satisfaction level from both parties' perspectives will depend on the willingness of each member to renegotiate the "terms" of their relationship. From Manuel's perspective, his wife's working outside the home or socializing with others, especially men, could be perceived as dishonorable. In Manuel's social network, his maleness (*machismo*) might be questioned and perceived as not having control over his wife. Manuel will have to be willing to deal with this and other social reactions if Yarette is to explore personal interests. Both new parents will soon realize that their lives are going to dramatically change, and to some degree "independence" or opportunities to pursue individual interests will become even more limited.

If both parties are willing to engage in this renegotiation, the counselor can serve as a facilitator for this dialogue. The counselor must exhibit *respeto* for Manuel's values and would benefit from reframing this negotiation process from a quest for Yarette's independence to an effort to help the family by strengthening of the marriage through the pursuit of personal interests. For example, as a result of feeling fulfilled, Yarette might not use alcohol to cope with her frustration, which clearly makes Yarette a better wife and mother. In addition, mutual personal interests that benefit both Manuel and Yarette should also be explored.

In my experience, when people are asked why they drink the usual response is "to relax" or "it is easier to talk to new people." Some problem drinkers will express that they drink to relieve depression or sadness. Then there are those who report that they drink because of frustration and boredom with their lives. Elements of Yarette's story, especially those related to not feeling allowed to pursue extracurricular activities in high school, lead me to believe that she is frustrated, bored, and generally understimulated. It appears that she knows there is something additional that life has to offer but feels constrained by rigid gender roles that are mediated by her culture.

A counselor should be knowledgeable about various cultural concepts and be willing to address the factors that compose the acculturation stress associated with being a first-generation Latina. Gender role expectations and the conflict between traditional family values and American culture will have to be negotiated and mediated. Because Latino culture emphasizes the family unit, the integration of supportive family members could facilitate this negotiation. In the Latino culture and unlike American culture in which responsibility is individualized, when one person has a problem it is everyone's problem. Therefore, the solution is truly a familial quest.

11. Addictions Counseling With Asian American Clients

■Critical Incident

Catherine Y. Chang

Background

Richard is a 17-year-old second-generation Asian American. His parents immigrated to the United States 19 years ago when his father, Jung, got a job as an engineer for a local industry. His father is semifluent in English but insists on speaking his native language at home. Although Richard's mother, Susan, understands the majority of spoken English, she speaks only broken English and speaks only her native language at home. Susan is a homemaker but occasionally will help out her friends who have a small business. She is active in their Presbyterian church and has limited friendships outside of the church. Hannah, Richard's 14-year-old sister, is a freshman in the same private school that Richard attends. She is shy, quiet, and a straight A student. Although both Richard and Hannah understand their native language, they have a difficult time speaking it fluently.

Richard is a senior who is active in student government and runs track. Until recently, he has been a straight A student all his life. Over the last quarter, however, his grades have dropped from all A's to C's and D's. Richard's hope had been to get into one of the top universities in the country. If his grades continue to drop, he will not get into his top universities. To the dismay of his parents, he has been going out every night with his friends and drinking behind his parents' back. He also has become disruptive in school and part of a group that received detention for instigating a food fight in the cafeteria. Additionally, Richard, along with the same group of individuals, was caught drinking at a school function. Despite his parents' disapproval, Richard has been dating a Caucasian girl for the past 3 months. Besides a few friends from church, Richard's friends are all "American."

Incident

On the basis of Richard's erratic behavior and drop in his school grades, the school counselor refers Richard and the Lee family to a community mental health agency. You are a White male counselor who is assigned this case. The reasons for the referral include acting-out behavior, dropping grades, and drinking. Richard recently was caught drinking at a school event.

Both parents and Richard are present for the first session. During the session, you observe that Jung, the father, does the majority of the talking and even responds to questions that you direct to Susan and Richard. You also observe that Susan and Jung converse in Korean before responding to your questions. You also observe that Richard is very aware of his father's responses and looks toward his father before responding.

In addition to the basic background information, you obtain the following from the initial session: Jung and Susan immigrated to the United States from Korea 19 years ago. Jung states that one of the primary reasons for leaving a very comfortable life in Korea was so his children would have a better education and a better life for themselves. His dream is for his children to grow up and be doctors or lawyers. The reason he works so much is so that they can attend the good private school and get into a good college. Susan agrees that this too is her dream. Jung also states that he is afraid that Richard is becoming "too American" and losing touch with traditional Korean values. He broke up with his "nice" Korean girlfriend and started dating "that wild American" girl.

With regard to familial relationships, Richard describes his relationship with his father as close, yet distant mainly because he works all the time. You note that it is important for Richard to obtain his father's approval. Richard describes his relationship with his mother as close. "She is always around when I need her." He describes his relationship with his sister as "typical." "She's 14."

When you inquire about Richard's drinking alcohol, Richard states, "It's not a big deal. Everybody including my father drinks. Father can't say anything about my drinking, because he has a DUI on his driving record." Richard also states that he has seen his father pass out several times in the past and his mother putting him to bed. You discover that Richard has been drinking regularly for the past 6 months. He drinks mainly when he's out with his "buddies." He does admit driving several times while intoxicated. When Jung is inquired about his drinking, he becomes very indignant and refuses to respond, stating that the only reason that they agreed to counseling was because the school counselor had suggested this as a way to help Richard with his grades.

Discussion

There are several salient issues that need to be considered in this case. The direction you take as a counselor will largely depend on your theoretical orientation and your understanding of multicultural and ethical issues. Particularly, you will want to consider issues related to acculturation, ethnic identity development, cultural values, and privilege and oppression. Additionally, you will want to consider that Asian Americans underutilize counseling services because of stigmatization of mental illness; therefore, it was likely very difficult for the Lee family to attend the first session. This will be important for you to consider in keeping the Lee family from premature termination.

Questions

1. What are the salient issues? How would you prioritize them in your approach to working with this family?
2. What modality of treatment would you choose for this case and why? What are your treatment goals and intervention strategies for this case?
3. How would you incorporate multicultural considerations in this case? As a White male counselor, what issues do you need to be aware of before working with this case?

■Response

Pamela S. Lassiter

After reading the case description, I am particularly struck by the family's willingness and courage to attend the first session and their apparent interest in each other as people. The fact that they showed up at all tells me that these parents are concerned about their son and that they are invested in his well-being. Richard's willingness to articulate his concerns for his father's drinking behavior (although not in a respectful way) and his nonverbal attachment to his father's reactions in session are positive indicators of systemic investment and give me much hope for change. A culturally competent and sensitive approach to the therapeutic process combined with the inherent competencies of this family sets the stage for a positive outcome.

In Question 1, the counselor is asked to outline the salient issues and to articulate how he might prioritize them in the process. The primary issues in this case appear to include potentially dangerous behavior, substance abuse or dependency with Richard and his father, generational acculturation and ethnic identity issues, attitudes and perspectives about mental health services, and family issues such as boundaries and communication patterns.

As in all situations related to teenage substance use, the counselor would likely want to prioritize an assessment of safety issues related to Richard's drinking and driving behaviors. Given the prevalence of teenage deaths due to driving under the influence, the old adage "safety first" definitely applies with this family. I would also want to know the extent of Richard's drinking as well as how aware his parents are of this situation.

Rapport building will be central to successful counseling with this family given the cultural issues involved. From a multicultural perspective, the counselor will need to address acculturation and ethnic identity issues (one's sense of group belongingness) early on in the process. This will give one the foundation for discussing other issues such as how the family views mental health services and even an evaluation of what type of counselor is most appropriate for working with this family. Acculturation occurs when two or more cultures interact and includes the process of adapting to a mainstream culture. The counselor will need to understand acculturation patterns generally associated with Asian families and, in this case, those issues specifically salient to Korean American families (see Chang & Myers, 1997). Counselors working with Korean American families will want to consider filial piety (respect for parent), group orientation (family group considerations take priority over the needs of the individual), restrained communication styles, and the value placed on academic achievement. With this family, acculturation appears to take on different meanings for different generations. The counselor will need to elicit these different generational meanings, have a clear understanding of the family's immigration history, and be aware of the potential barriers to mental health services related to ethnic identity and acculturation. Several studies suggest that Asian Americans underuse mental health services and terminate early despite a greater need for such services (Atkinson & Gim, 1989; Atkinson, Whiteley, & Gim, 1990; Gim, Atkinson, & Whiteley, 1990; Leong, 1994). Some barriers to consider may include language issues, biases inherent in the mental health system primarily oriented toward English-speaking Caucasian clients, a belief that disclosing personal problems to a professional may be viewed as disgraceful, lack of counselor training in Asian cultural issues, and counselor bias against Asian clients.

In addition to multicultural considerations, the counselor will need to address general substance abuse counseling issues. First things first. What are the presenting concerns of the family? What was the reason for referral? What factors (or who) made this family follow through with the first appointment? Who is most concerned about Richard's behavior? When did his behavior begin to change and what does the family attribute to the change? In terms of substance abuse, the following questions seem relevant, What is the extent of Richard's alcohol/other drug use? How does it impair his functioning? How many of his peers are active in their use of substances? Does Richard's behavior have hidden or deeper meanings for the family as a whole? Although initially the counselor does not have "permission" to delve into Jung's drinking behavior, it has been stated in the room by Richard and will need exploration later as the counselor continues to establish rapport and goes through those issues the family is comfortable addressing early in the process. Other relevant issues for exploration at a later time include familial boundaries and communication barriers.

In Question 2, the counselor is asked to consider the preferred treatment modality for this scenario as well as treatment goals and strategies. The modality chosen for this case is largely dependent on the counselor's theoretical orientation and training as well as the mission of the agency. A preferred option is family counseling because the concerns seem to affect all family members and the presenting issues appear to be supported by the dynamics within the system. Although individual counseling or group counseling for Richard may be an effective intervention, it would seem to exclude the concerns he stated in the initial interview about his father's substance use and the intergenerational issues around acculturation.

General treatment goals and intervention strategies to consider include the following:

- **To ensure the safety of Richard and to assess the severity of substance abuse**
  Assess drinking and driving
  Assess amount and frequency of alcohol and other drug use, including the role of peer influence and the effect on overall functioning
- **To assess general family functioning**
  Examine communication patterns between children and parents
  Examine parental knowledge of extent of Richard's substance use
  Evaluate ongoing assessment of father's substance use and effect on family
- **To increase Richard's overall functioning both in school and at home**
  Increase peer and familial support around acculturation issues
- **To improve the relationship between child and parent**
  Enhance communication skills and respect among family members
  Define and establish family hierarchy/boundaries, respecting cultural contexts of those hierarchies

Although I have suggested the father's substance use/abuse as an issue in treatment, caution should be used in addressing this issue too directly or too quickly. Challenging the father too soon risks losing the family before trust and rapport can be adequately established. Going through the parents' concerns about their son will be a more effective way to eventually address the father's issues and is consistent with recommendations from the literature about culturally competent counseling with Asian Americans. A metaphor for conceptualization might be to think of a flower bed a gardener is preparing for the spring planting. To encourage blooming later, one should first prepare and nurture the soil. Establishing a safe, culturally sensitive therapeutic atmosphere early in the process will likely lay the foundation for significant growth later.

In Question 3, the counselor is asked to incorporate multicultural competency with his own cultural background. In working with minority clients, it is not so much about doing things differently, but more about doing things a little slower and with more intention or purpose. You may have to spend a considerable amount of time building rapport and explaining how the mental health system works. For example, some Asian clients may have no knowledge about the role and function of a professional counselor. Many Asians seek the advice of other family members or clergy when needing assistance with personal matters. The idea of paying a total stranger to listen to your problems may seem contrary to many Asians who believe in emotional restraint. A counselor will need to inform the Asian family about the role of the counselor, the counseling process, and the role of the client family in that process—keeping in mind that the degree of information needed will vary depending on the client's level of acculturation and ethnic identity development. In this case, it will take an artful balance of information sharing and respect for natural resistance to counseling to keep the family engaged in the process.

As a White counselor or as a counselor of any racial background, you will need to be mindful of your own cultural values and biases. A part of this would include your awareness and understanding of oppression and privilege issues—especially as a White male counselor who is a member of two visible majority groups. The impact of the various identities brought into the counseling room by the counselor can be used consciously to facilitate change. For example, some Asian clients may give a White male counselor a great deal of referential power. They may believe the counselor is in a higher position because of their professional status and professional knowledge. Song (1999) suggested that the counselor can use this hierarchical structure to join with the client. Some Korean American clients may actually prefer a structured, directive, paternalistic, or even authoritarian approach to counseling (Chang & Myers, 1997). Korean Americans tend to be family oriented, value harmony and emotional restraint, and subscribe to well-defined hierarchical role structures. Establishing treatment goals that are family oriented and child focused rather than individual oriented may prove to be more acceptable and productive (Song, 1999). Additionally, many Asian clients may expect quick diagnosis and treatment benefit early on in the counseling process (Huang, 1994), so focusing on symptom relief in the early stages may be helpful.

The previous suggestions are based on clinical experience and literature on counseling Asian American clients. It is crucial that counselors not fall into the trap of stereotyping their clients. Asian Americans are a heterogeneous group, and while there are some commonalties among groups, it is important not to overgeneralize cultural knowledge and values. Instead, counselors should seek to understand the individual background of each client or family, including the uniqueness that comes from considering one's country of origin, generation status, language, and ethnic group. One way to maintain cultural sensitivity and to avoid stereotyping will be to remain actively engaged in ongoing supervision and consultation that challenges and expands your cultural awareness and biases that will naturally come from your own background.

■References

Atkinson, D. R., & Gim, R. H. (1989). Asian-American cultural identity and attitudes toward mental health services. *Journal of Counseling Psychology, 36,* 209–212.

Atkinson, D. R., Whiteley, S., & Gim, R. H. (1990). Asian-American acculturation and preferences for health providers. *Journal of College Student Development, 31,* 155–161.

Chang, C., & Myers, J. (1997). Understanding and counseling Korean Americans: Implications for training. *Counselor Education and Supervision, 37,* 35–49.

Gim, R. H., Atkinson, D. R., & Whiteley, S. (1990). Asian-American acculturation, severity of concerns, and willingness to see a counselor. *Journal of Counseling Psychology, 37,* 281–285.

Huang, L. N. (1994). An integrative approach to clinical assessment and intervention with Asian-American adolescents. *Journal of Clinical Child Psychology, 23,* 21–31.

Leong, F. (1994). Asian Americans' differential patterns of utilization of inpatient and outpatient public mental health services in Hawaii. *Journal of Community Psychology, 22,* 82–96.

Song, S. J. (1999). Using solution-focused therapy with Korean families. In K. S. Ng (Ed.), *Counseling Asian families from a systems perspective* (pp. 127–141). Alexandria, VA: American Counseling Association.

12
Addiction Among the Native American Population

Critical Incident

Michael Tlanusta Garrett

Background

Will is a 41-year-old Native American man who lives in a metropolitan area and works for a finance company during the day and as a DJ at a local radio station during the evenings. Like so many Native American families that were relocated to urban areas during the 1950s and 1960s, Will's family moved from the reservation to the city. The family followed Will's father, who had been a part of the U.S. government's relocation program to find work following his return from military service. Will's father worked as a welder to support his family, and he drank heavily in his spare time. He was known to have a temper when he drank, and although Will reports that his father never showed violence toward the family, he had quite a reputation for bar fights and short-term jail time. Will reports that his father had a major influence on him "both in a good way and in a bad way at the same time."

Although born on the reservation, Will remembers very little of it from his childhood before moving to the city. Will went to school in the city and made infrequent trips back to the reservation where some family remained. He was a popular guy who did not have the best of grades but who, during high school, excelled in athletics, hoping for a scholarship that never materialized. Upon graduating from high school, he married his high school sweetheart and took up work for a while with a local contractor who was a friend of his father. Soon thereafter, Will's first son was born, and Will describes the event as "one of the best things that's ever happened" to him. As a dedicated father, he desperately wanted to "do better" for his family, so he enrolled in the local community college where he attended part time. Not long after receiving his associate degree, Will's second son was born. Will was fortunate to take a job with a local finance company where he worked his way up quickly with a combination of skill, expertise, and "great people know-how." Everything seemed to be going well for Will and his family until his father was tragically killed in a car accident that was later found to be alcohol related.

Will had drunk socially in high school but usually kept it to a minimum because it affected his "performance on the field." Following his father's death, however, Will began drinking frequently and intensely, though initially never enough to keep him from being able to handle his day-to-day routines. It was clear to everyone around him, however, that Will was acting different, more forgetful, and just plain distant. This went on for some time and did not come to a head until one day, when Will's wife called him and asked him to pick up the boys from their after-school activities. Will, who had gotten off work early that day and had been drinking, went to pick the boys up in an intoxicated state and ended up running off the side of the road. Although no one was hurt, it scared Will and his sons so much that he voluntarily entered a treatment program and began attending AA. However, amid the strain of so many things going on and a fairly shaky marriage for more than a few years, Will and his wife divorced, and she kept primary custody of the two boys, whom he sees on a regular basis.

Will went through a period of deep introspection and long string of short-term relationships with a number of women who, as Will describes it, were interested in him because he was American Indian. Always, though, it came down to the same thing in his mind—their disillusionment with realizing that Will did not fit the stereotyped spiritual image of what an American Indian was supposed to be. However, at that same time, Will started taking more of an interest in his Native American culture and attended a number of powwows held in the local area.

Before long, Will was not only attending such cultural events on a regular basis but became very active through participation on the planning committees as well. He also became active in the local metropolitan Indian organization and even took some of the dance classes held there, typically directed at the children. As an enrolled member of his tribe, Will was soon competing in some of the smaller powwows in the traditional dance category and faired well at it. In addition to his proficiency in dance, Will also took up the Native flute and became quite proficient in that as well. He even cut a CD through some help with coworkers at the radio station.

As Will's immersion into his culture continued, he began to really question a lot of the process and underlying philosophy of AA. During one of the meetings, he even got into a pretty heated debate with a fellow member that resulted in Will deciding he would not participate anymore with "people who didn't understand the traditional way." Not long after, Will began spending some weekends back on the reservation where he learned from one of the medicine men there, participating in ceremony through medicine sweats. During one of the ceremonies, Will was honored to receive his traditional name and had been completely sober ever since, taking great pride in his walking the "Good Red Road." That was 5 years ago. More recently, however, Will started having a string of bad dreams that coincided with a continued string of bad relationships and has not been able to sleep. He admits that many of his dreams are about his father. He also started drinking again.

Incident

Will comes for crisis counseling, looking very disheveled and distraught. He describes a scenario in which, earlier that day, he had been standing alone staring out the window of his suburban apartment with a .45 caliber handgun pointed at his head. He admits that he has battled alcoholism for many years now and according to him, it has cost him almost everything he loves most in life. He has fought to be a good father to his two young sons. He has grappled all his life with "an emptiness," as he describes it, deep down in his spirit, and that constant nagging urge to always take another drink. He has been in and out of treatment programs, on and off with AA, and now he just wants all the pain to stop. He describes feeling the coldness of the barrel against his throbbing temple, and as he stares out of the window at the beautiful summer day unfolding before him, he notices a little turtle struggling to go from one place to another. Then he notices the cat crouched not far away from the turtle waiting for the right moment to pounce on its helpless prey. The turtle, spying the cat in waiting, quickly pulls into its shell. Just then, the cat leaps toward the turtle, pawing and hissing. Safely in its shell, the turtle remains unharmed by the persistent cat, which tries to open this troublesome package, knocking it upside down, prying, but to no avail. Frustrated, the cat wanders off in search of easier prey. Moments pass before the turtle emerges slowly from the safety of its shell once again. First the head, then a leg or two, and finally everything back where it was. The turtle, which is lying upside down from the ordeal, slowly pushes itself with one leg, flips himself back right side up, and continues on his journey. Will, who has become so engrossed in this drama taking place before him, has lowered the gun from his head as he continues to watch. The turtle comes to a log. Will looks on, expecting the turtle to find some way to go around this barrier, but the turtle just slowly, patiently climbs over the log and flips down on the other side of it. As Will glances down at the gun in his hand, his eyes begin to swell with tears. As he looks back out the window, the turtle has disappeared.

Questions

1. What is the best way to process the incident just described by Will in a way that would be culturally responsive and therapeutically beneficial?
2. What should be a next step for working with Will to address his short-term needs? Long-term needs?
3. What role, if any, should a traditional Native American healer (i.e., medicine man or woman) play in provision of services to Will?
4. What is the best way to address Will's spiritual dilemma within the context of his alcohol addiction?

■Response

Kenneth M. Coll

When counselors are confronted with a client and situation like this, it is important to consider cultural context. The mental health issues of American Indian/

Alaskan Natives (AI/AN) might be best understood in the context of historical wounding, the impact of historical events, and social context on the multigenerational psychological and behavioral patterns of individuals. Moane (1994) noted that there are psychological patterns inherited from colonization that may be transmitted through family dynamics. Though controlled research on historical wounding is elusive, Moane proposed that colonialism relies on mechanisms of control, including physical coercion, sexual exploitation, economic exploitation, political exclusion, and control of ideology and culture. These mechanisms leave a psychological legacy, including dependency, fear, ambivalence toward the colonizer, suppression of anger and rage, a sense of inferiority, self-hatred, loss of identity, horizontal violence, and vulnerability to psychological distress. While the specific multigenerational psychological impact is largely unknown, it is understood to be a root cause of the suffering of Indian people and as a contributing factor for high rates of alcoholism, depression, suicide, and domestic abuse. In light of this context, very relevant questions are posed related to culturally competent treatment for Will.

Processing the Incident/Culturally Responsive

Related to Question 1, it is of paramount importance to provide crisis counseling and/or hospitalization until Will's acute suicidal ideation and behaviors have abated. Relapse is often a trigger for a downward spiral into hopelessness and despair. As such, stabilization is of vital importance. Perhaps one way to assist stabilization and deescalation of suicidal thought is to briefly discuss the "turtle" incident, probing what it symbolizes for Will, accenting the incident's message of hope, and then facilitating the planning of further exploration of this incident with a traditional healer.

Short-Term Needs/Long-Term Needs

In the short term, and especially as a non-AI/AN counselor, it would be important to assess the following counseling process issues in working with Will to ensure culturally competent interactions: assumptions about AI/AN people and ongoing clarification with Will about specific AI/AN context and cultural nuances.

Critical incidents in Will's life also need to be noted and explored. For example, unresolved grief and loss issues (father's death, breakup of Will's family) seem very important. In addition, an asset search and discussion could be helpful. For example, Will seems to be a caring and dedicated father. Other strengths include connecting with his culture and his talents in music and dance.

Longer term, assessing and working with Will's level of acculturation is vital. Garrett and Pichette (2000) noted that for Native American people, living in a metropolitan area and not being raised in the traditional ways often can create a great deal of internal conflict, leading to internalization of anger. According to Garrett and Pichette, Will's level of acculturation is probably "marginal," meaning Will is in a seemingly no-win cultural situation, caught between two

Critical Incidents in Addictions Counseling

cultures. Being caught between two worlds is considered a "danger zone" and suggests a deep struggle for identity and a sense of place. Certainly this describes Will's state of mind and current situation. Talking about such issues, in coordination with a traditional healer/medicine person, could prove fruitful.

Another area to explore is the extent of Will's relational worldview (Garrett & Pichette, 2000). The relational worldview concept accents interpersonal relationships and highly respects responsibility toward others. Garrett indicated that many AI/AN people define themselves less on possessions and more on family ties and traditional customs and beliefs. He noted that with such a strong cultural emphasis on one's relationship with others (especially extended family), AI/AN people can be susceptible to encountering a variety of difficulties (including depression) in a society that emphasizes individualism, competition, and achievement over contrasting values of group harmony, cooperation, and sharing. There are indications that Will embraces this traditional AI/AN value system. Therefore, helping him understand the conflicts this system has with the mainstream society and assisting him in building deeper relationships with his sons and others (extended family, relatives) are very important to Will's recovery process.

Role of the Traditional Healer

Will needs to be queried extensively about his wishes concerning culturally specific healing. As Manson (2001) noted, traditional healing is common in many AI/AN communities, with ethnographic studies indicating that traditional healing does indeed help such problems as depression and substance-related disorders. Moreover, traditional healing approaches frequently operate in cooperation with Western psychotherapeutic interventions. With Will's consent and involvement, working collaboratively and cooperatively with traditional healer(s) should be emphasized. For example, helping Will reconnect with his sons and perhaps teaching them about their identity as Native American people could be one collaborative effort. Ceremonies and ongoing traditional practices appropriate to Will's tribal affiliation and beliefs (e.g., sweat lodge purification) specifically can address Will's recent bad dreams, suicidal behavior, and sense of emptiness. A discussion and perhaps ceremony with a traditional healer related to Will's turtle experience would also be important.

Ways to Address the Spiritual Dilemma

In response to Question 4, AA is based on Christian constructs and therefore may not be the best spiritual healing fit for Will. Or perhaps a combination of traditional spirituality and AA may work in ongoing healing and relapse prevention. Such ideas need to be explored and discussed.

In conclusion, I would like to reiterate that I believe the right questions have been asked to elicit the best help for Will. The described case involves circumstances that create a myriad of issues that have the potential of impacting effective treatment and recovery. As a Lakota traditional healer asserted, "We need our healing ways. Without them, I don't think we have much of a chance of getting ahead of what alcoholism has done to our people" (Arbogast, 1996, p. 318).

References

Arbogast, D. (1996) *Wounded warriors: A time for healing.* Omaha, NE: Little Turtle Publications.

Garrett, M. T., & Pichette, E. F. (2000). Red as an apple: Native American acculturation and counseling with or without reservation. *Journal of Counseling & Development, 78,* 3–13.

Manson, S. (2001). Behavioral health services for American Indians. In M. Dixon & Y. Roubideaux (Eds.), *Promises to keep: Public health policy for American Indians and Alaska Natives in the 21st century* (pp. 174–185). Washington, DC: American Public Health Association.

Moane, G. (1994). A psychological analysis of colonialism in an Irish context. *Irish Journal of Psychology, 15,* 250–265.

13 Counseling Clients With Eating Disorders

■Critical Incident

Courtenay Trahan

Background

Amanda is a 20-year-old Caucasian college student. She is a social work major at a private Catholic university in an affluent area. Amanda is the oldest of three. She has a brother and sister, both in high school. Amanda reports that her parents are happily married, although since she has left for college, her mother has become increasingly depressed. When questioned about the depression, she states that her mother now has trouble getting out of bed, the house is a mess, and she no longer cooks for the family. Amanda states that her relationship with her father is good. When asked for more detail about the relationship, Amanda reports that her father is mainly interested in how she is doing in school. This has been a theme for their relationship all her life. Amanda is a nurturer. She often goes home and cleans and cooks for the family.

Amanda came to the university's counseling office desperate for help. She self-referred, writing on her intake that her main issues were low self-esteem, difficulty with relationships, and weight control (this being her primary concern). In our sessions together, Amanda shared that she has had a problem with overeating for years. As our conversation progressed, Amanda shared that she often eats alone in her room because of embarrassment over the amount of food she eats. She stated that she regularly keeps food hidden in her apartment. In addition, she disclosed that she would buy two of the same item at the grocery store and eat the duplicates in the car on the way home. Furthermore, Amanda stated that she limits herself socially to avoid seeing other people. She reports that the idea of dating and meeting new people creates anxiety for her.

Two recurrent themes emerged throughout our sessions together. Amanda repeatedly made the statement, "If I were thinner, I would be happier." In addition, Amanda expressed an overwhelming desire to be "perfect," especially in the area of academics.

Incident

At the time of the incident Amanda and I had been working together for approximately 5 months. I received a phone message from Amanda the day the university opened after spring break requesting an emergency appointment. I met with Amanda that afternoon. Over the break Amanda went to her family doctor for a physical. During the appointment she was weighed by her physician and was told that she needed to lose weight. She reported bursting into tears in front of her doctor and sharing with him some of her struggles with her weight. He wrote her a prescription for Paxil and asked her to follow up in 3 weeks. On her way home she stopped off at a store and bought $100 worth of groceries, then drove her car to a secluded spot in a neighborhood park. Amanda reported that she had no memory of what happened next. The next thing she was able to remember was seeing food wrappers strewn all over the front seat. Amanda stated this was the most out of control she had ever been. This incident occurred 3 days prior to my session with her. During our session Amanda mentioned for the first time that she was having some suicidal thoughts. I conducted a thorough suicide assessment and asked Amanda to sign a contract agreeing to call for help before taking any action that might cause self-harm. Finally, I referred Amanda to an eating disorder group on campus, to provide added support from her peers and the group facilitator.

Discussion

Amanda continued with our sessions and began to go to the weekly eating disorder group meetings. Over the next few weeks Amanda and I used cognitive-behavioral strategies to combat her eating concerns, mainly her feelings of guilt and shame around eating. She began to keep a food diary, documenting how she felt before and after eating. We also worked on self-esteem issues and worked toward challenging her belief that she would be happier if she were thinner. By the end of the semester, it seemed that the antidepressant medication was providing some relief for Amanda, and she had decided to join Weight Watchers over the summer to continue to receive support in this area. We also developed a crisis plan that Amanda could implement in the event that she felt out of control or suicidal. Amanda did not return to school in the fall. Unfortunately, her mother's depression worsened and she was hospitalized. Amanda made the choice to stay home and take classes locally to help care for her family.

Questions

1. Are there interventions or strategies that the counselor could have implemented prior to the incident, possibly even preventing it?
2. Should the counselor have referred Amanda to the university's health services office to be put on antidepressants earlier in the timeline of their sessions?

3. Once the counselor found out that Amanda was not returning to school, would it have been appropriate to call and check to see how she was doing and perhaps facilitate a referral?

∎Response

Kelly M. Burch-Ragan

Effectively working with people suffering from eating disorders can be particularly challenging. Unlike intervening in alcohol or drug addictions, the option to either be free from the abusive substance or not is simply not an option; our bodies must have food and water to survive. However, like alcohol and drug abuse, binge eating can progress to the level of addiction. People who compulsively overeat may be a few hundred pounds overweight or only a few pounds. The key to successful intervention is not related to how much a person weighs but the person's reasons for eating.

Additionally, people like Amanda, who binge/overeat, are confronted and frequently accept a language of personal deficit ascribed to them within a larger social context. From a narrative perspective, counselors can facilitate and disrupt a client's deficit-based beliefs and challenge the dominant discourse surrounding and nurturing the life of the problem. This response does not reject the usefulness of deficit-based approaches. Indeed, the intent of this response is an appreciation of "both/and" thinking, thereby creating space in therapeutic practice that invites strength-based narratives and shifts in perspective that heal.

There is no single cause supporting compulsive eating/binging behavior. Effectively working with people challenged by food issues is a reflexive and interrelated process. It involves deconstructing food's place in Amanda's relationship with others, deconstructing the claim that food placed on Amanda's identity, renegotiating the place of food in Amanda's life, renegotiating Amanda's relationship with food once she is free from its domination, and finally renegotiating Amanda's relationships with others.

Amanda's counselor clearly demonstrates the knowledge and clinical skill to address the dynamics that invite Amanda to participate in binge eating. The counselor's attention to Amanda's intake assessment created not only a venue by which to further understand the progression and state of Amanda's clinical disorder but also an opportunity to discover the discourse nurturing Amanda's stated primary concern, "weight control." Further, the counselor identified key themes, often referred to as myths, that are commonly associated with people struggling with binge eating. Perfectionism and a belief that an external change will bring a lasting sense of happiness can be alluring myths to perpetuate the life of the problem.

The counselor's first question illustrates the hope of many helping professionals of quality—the desire to intervene in a manner that counteracts the life-sustaining force of the problem (negative feedback loops) and potentially prevents life-threatening consequences. The counselor's use of cognitive-behavioral strategies, support groups, interdisciplinary intervention, a suicide assessment, and a signed contract that Amanda agreed to seek help before acting in a self-injurious manner was exactly on target following the incident. While many of these strategies might have been useful prior to the incident, it is quite likely that Amanda would not have been receptive to such interventions earlier in therapy, particularly given that she views herself as the "nurturer" and "weight control" is her primary concern. Furthermore, during the first 5 months of therapy, the counselor established a trusting relationship with Amanda, thereby opening the door to understanding key discourses and relational perspectives that might prove invaluable to eventually unraveling the complex, intertwining influential factors of Amanda's struggle.

The counselor successfully opened several potentially relevant and yet-to-be challenged discourses. Challenging the underlying assumptions and socially dominant stories creates space for alternative, multidimensional change to occur. The journey to desired change for Amanda might include focusing on several concepts that, once challenged, promote the creation of helpful alternatives through counseling. For example, Amanda might be constrained by cultural pressures to be thin. The "anxiety" created by "dating and meeting new people" could be Amanda's subconscious desire to protect herself from love and intimacy. Amanda's binge-eating behavior also could be a form of self-medication to alleviate the anxiety. Physiologically, eating causes the blood sugar to rise and arouses the brain's production of endorphins. In either case, the physiological impact is one of relaxation. Amanda's anxiety could support her binge-eating behavior in an effort to feel "normal." Another contributing factor might be the use of food to relieve stress (e.g., her worries over her mother's depression) or depression (e.g., Amanda's intake assessment indicating low self-esteem and familial history of depression). Or Amanda might be utilizing food to express a need for control, which is not an infrequent occurrence among people dominated by the myth of perfectionism. Amanda expressed a tremendous desire to be "perfect, especially in the area of academics." It stands to reason that there may be a damaging connection between Amanda's desire to be academically "perfect" and her "good" relationship with her father, which has a lifelong foundation in "how she is doing in school." While food may become the battleground for control, in reality, if this discourse rings true for Amanda, food is in control and robbing her of quality and possibly her life.

The aforementioned aspects of individual, familial, and larger social practices are intricately connected. Discerning the relevant elements that place restraints on Amanda's successful recovery and collaboratively forming new and helpful relationships between Amanda, herself, her family, dominant social norms, and others are not easy tasks. The matter is complicated by biological processes that are best addressed in collaboration with other helping professionals (e.g., medical treatment, antidepressant medication and management).

In Question 2, the counselor seems to be evaluating the timing of his or her approach to Amanda's treatment. Eating disorders, like other types of addictive/

abusive behaviors, often demand the expertise of an interdisciplinary team of helping professionals. And hindsight is almost always 20/20. Amanda sought help from the appropriate place, counseling, for reflexive examination of her problem. The presentation of her problem was, no doubt, as Amanda honestly viewed it primarily a "weight control" issue. Meeting, respecting, and appreciating the expertise of counseling clients is not simple. Counselors must carefully balance their own knowledge and expertise in a particular area while respecting the voice of the client and assessing a client's readiness and willingness to entertain alternative perspectives and interventions from other helping providers.

While Amanda's intake revealed several behaviors commonly associated with depression (e.g., anxiety, isolation, low self-esteem), there was no definitive indication that Amanda's problem demanded immediate interaction with other helping professionals. Nonetheless, it is better to err on the side of caution. Referral to a medical expert to rule out contributing biological factors is prudent and protective of the client's health and well-being. Approaching the interdisciplinary intervention in such a manner presents a vehicle for balancing the complex dynamics of providing help, particularly in the field of eating-disordered behaviors.

My response to Question 3 is an absolute affirmative. The counselor is right on track with making referrals and checking on how Amanda is doing. As counselors, it is our ethical duty to protect the welfare of our clients and foster their independence. There is a huge difference between demonstrating professional regard through follow-up calls and referrals and using interventions that undermine a client's autonomy. The counselor may discover that Amanda has already made contact with additional support systems and referral sources. In which case, the counselor affirms Amanda's proactive actions. Or the counselor may find that he or she needs to locate and make referrals for Amanda. Neither is good or bad. It is simply a matter of continuum of care, ethical practice, and simultaneously facilitating closure while positively contributing to the creation of new alternatives. This counselor clearly established a trusting and productively working therapeutic relationship with Amanda. This relationship can serve as the bridge to Amanda's continued desired change.

In conclusion, I restate that eating-disordered behaviors are fraught with complex, intertwined issues. There is not a simple path to follow; each client deserves individualized care that honors the client's expertise as well as the knowledge gained from professional research and outcome studies. Amanda's counselor demonstrated this type of care. The counselor's willingness to question and be open to alternative thoughts and interventions strongly suggests a commitment to lifelong learning and providing quality care that may improve the counselor's future counseling interventions in the field of eating disorders and his or her transitional contact with Amanda.

14

Older Adults and the Issue of Addiction

■Critical Incident

Laura J. Veach

Background

There are major differences in addiction treatment settings from 20 years ago. Residential care was the primary mode of care for most individuals diagnosed with addiction in the 1980s. Currently, the primary level of care used to treat addiction is an intensive outpatient level of care. Much has been documented about the continued efficacy of intensive outpatient treatment for addiction. Yet, there are some clients who need a greater intensity of care in a residential treatment setting for addiction. In particular, when an older adult (a person over age 55) is admitted to a residential level of care, very often either the client has been considered unsuccessful after multiple admissions to intensive outpatient levels of care or the client has significant medical and other mental health issues such that admission to intensive outpatient care levels are con-traindicated. The number of older adults in the United States is increasing rapidly. More older adults are seeking treatment for chemical dependency as noted in recent reports from the Office of Applied Studies in the Substance Abuse and Mental Health Services Administration (SAMHSA), which indi-cated there were 58,000 admissions of older adults in 2001, with almost two thirds exclusively due to alcohol problems (U.S. Department of Health and Human Services, 2004). Residential addiction treatment is more often recom-mended for the treatment of addiction in older adults, often because of greater medical and emotional complications that cannot be adequately addressed in an outpatient setting.

Incident

Just this year, Carl, a 74-year-old recently widowed client, was admitted to our residential program. Carl had a significantly elevated blood alcohol level (BAL) on admission of .44, a level that could cause overdose and death in a person without a high tolerance to alcohol. Most people when admitted, if inebriated, have a BAL of between .10 and .30. Older adults with a long history of drinking often have a higher BAL upon admission and need more careful medical detoxification and monitoring.

Carl was obviously inebriated on admission with such an elevated BAL, but he was able to talk and sit in a chair. He agreed to being admitted for addiction treatment. Information about Carl obtained from his adult children on admission confirmed that he had been a drinker over the past 25 years and had three previous treatment episodes for alcohol dependency, with the most recent occurring 10 years prior to the current admission. His longest period of sobriety, 9 years, followed the last admission. The medical team was involved in immediate and continued close monitoring of Carl's withdrawal, medical detoxification, and preexisting diagnosis of hypertension. The medical team communicated extensively with Carl's attending physician to coordinate appropriate medical interventions to help Carl carefully stabilize.

My initial contact with Carl as his primary counselor during his days of medical detoxification was limited to brief individual sessions and developing rapport. I utilized techniques involving reminiscing to build rapport and begin to understand Carl's life story. He was tearful at times as he recounted the loss of his wife the previous year when their home was destroyed by fire. He attributed the loss of his wife as the triggering event leading to his relapse with alcohol.

Discussion

Because of significant issues related to the death of Carl's wife of 35 years, special attention was given to his grief and loss and other major life transitions. In addition, as his medical stabilization occurred over the next 5 days, and his cognitive functioning improved, Carl began to attend psychoeducational groups. This initial care included a focus on socialization as a means of assisting Carl in processing his grief. In addition, group participation allowed Carl to begin to experience therapeutic factors of universality, instillation of hope, and a decrease in isolation.

Our program has an initial care phase specifically for those who are in their 1st week of care led by an initial care counselor. The family members are asked to attend this group with the client so there can be a foundation of information and orientation to treatment that is shared by the client, their family, and the treatment team. This initial care phase is also designed to provide other therapeutic benefits. For example, small group meetings in which issues arising in the early stages of those contemplating change can be addressed. In addition, regular family meetings are initiated in an attempt to decrease distortion in what might be communicated between the identified client and family members involved in the person's care. Finally, during this phase of treatment, individualized evaluation and assessment of client needs occurs in a more focused manner by the clinical team.

Carl responded well to encouragement to attend the initial care groups beginning in his 4th day of detoxification. Two of his four adult children attended the initial care phase groups. Carl was able to express fears about returning to his current home environment without drinking. Carl and his adult children shared their concerns about the difficulties Carl experienced after relocating to a new neighborhood in a condominium since the fire that destroyed the family home of 20 years. As I continued to meet with Carl and his family in several sessions, we began to outline important areas for individual, group, and family counseling as Carl entered the intensive phase of his treatment. After repeated encouragement, however, his adult children declined to attend the intensive family groups offered once per week citing busy schedules.

Following his successful detoxification, Carl joined in the primary intensive group and I was his primary counselor for the group. This was the beginning of his first days without any chemicals since the death of his wife the previous year. It is believed that active addiction interferes with successfully progressing through the stages of grief, and so it became primarily important for grief as well as sobriety issues to be addressed. Over the next 3 weeks, Carl made significant progress in joining in the group and processing the grief issues around his significant losses, namely, his wife of 35 years in a tragic fire, his home of 20 years, the familiarity of his neighborhood, his gardening hobbies since his new condominium had no community gardening space, and most recently, his sobriety. Carl was an active group member; he reestablished his support relationship with his 12-step sponsor, stabilized medically, and shared substantial progress as he prepared for discharge from the residential facility.

Six months after discharge from the residential facility, I was contacted by one of Carl's children. She informed me that Carl had died earlier that week after suffering a fall in his condominium. He sustained severe head injuries from the fall, and his autopsy revealed he had a .40 BAL. She shared that her siblings knew Carl had been drinking on a few occasions, but since they had not witnessed any significant episodes of intoxication, they were not overly concerned and had not talked with anyone about their father's recent drinking.

Questions

1. What should the primary addiction counselor do in order to deal with this kind of information?
2. What counseling recommendations might she make to the family? What other recommendations or interventions by the primary counselor might have helped this family better deal with issues pertaining to an older adult with addiction issues?
3. What does the counselor need to do to process her clinical decisions with the treatment facility? With her supervisor? With her peer supervision group?

Response

Richard Madwid

In this case of Carl, I support the direction of the primary counselor working with the loss of Carl's wife of 35 years as an entry point of treatment. Oftentimes, counselors trained to help clients label triggers that lead to relapse do not spend sufficient time with grief/loss issues such as Carl's. I was impressed by the primary counselor's focus on this issue, as well as on other life transitions. Though not mentioned, examples of issues that may be present for Carl might include managing bills and finances, arranging transportation, managing his household, maintaining his social life, arranging for medical care, and so forth.

Addiction treatment by way of utilizing models of addiction and family history also requires a close examination of the client's age with attention to developmental characteristics that may impact the addiction as well as other life challenges. In treating Carl's addiction, the primary counselor respected and considered developmental features of the case in the initial phase.

In response to Question 1, I believe the primary counselor was very supportive of Carl and his adult children. The primary counselor repeatedly encouraged Carl's adult children to attend the intensive family groups. Once again, the primary counselor accurately assessed that sobriety and assisting Carl's grief process went hand in hand. If Carl's adult children could have participated in this level of work, Carl might have experienced increased success in stabilizing.

Upon hearing about Carl's death from one of Carl's children, it would be important for the counselor to continue to offer support and recommend grief counseling by providing a specific referral to their geographic area. Carl's children could be experiencing guilt over not talking with anyone about their father's recent drinking and the high alcohol level disclosed upon his death. In addition, the primary counselor might be experiencing feelings of loss or inadequacy as a result of the contact by one of Carl's children. If this is the case, it should be discussed in clinical supervision.

In response to Question 2, as previously stated, recommendations to the family might include a referral for grief and loss counseling. Some areas have groups for family members, or perhaps an individual counselor who specializes in grief/loss counseling. If the residential facility where Carl lived has these outpatient services, this might provide the better choice because of the connection made to the facility during Carl's treatment.

Other recommendations or interventions the primary counselor might have utilized to assist the family to better deal with an older adult with an addiction could be considered. These could include the following:

1. Developing an after-care plan with Carl's family to support and monitor Carl's recovery. This plan could clearly address roles and responsibilities of all the adult children on a daily to weekly basis. The plan would be very specific as to the needs of Carl (i.e., daily phone contact, visits, shopping, assistance in household management). The plan would also focus on all family members with Carl getting continued counseling regarding grief and loss issues.
2. Linking family members with outreach programs for older adults such as Meals On Wheels to lessen the burden on family members for daily

Critical Incidents in Addictions Counseling

needs. Other outreach linkages might be to agencies that offer counselors to provide home visits for individual or family therapy.

3. A thorough review of the 9 years of sobriety that Carl achieved would be most important. It can be very helpful for counselors to help families assess what works, as described within the solution-focused model of counseling.

Finally, in response to Question 3, the processing of clinical decisions might best be done in the context of a team. Although this appears so basic to the treatment of addictions, it needs to be reiterated and examined. In addition, clinical decisions should be assessed regularly by a qualified, trained supervisor. The counselor in this case needs to seek out this consistency of supervision and communicate regarding the case with peers and supervisors to maximize the use of recommendations and feedback.

■Reference

U.S. Department of Health and Human Services. (2004, May). *The DASIS report: Older adults in substance abuse treatment: 2001.* Retrieved October 27, 2004, from http://oas.samhsa.gov/2k4/olderAdultsTX/olderAdultsTX.htm

15
Counseling the Court-Mandated Addict

■Critical Incident

Kelly L. Wester

Background

Jermaine is a 15-year-old African American male who lives with his 56-year-old grandmother who is legally blind, his three sisters ranging in age from 12 to 16, and a 4-year-old cousin. Jermaine has lived with his grandmother, Betsy, for the past 3 years. Betsy has legal custody of him and the rest of the children since their parents have all been in prison for various reasons. Jermaine's father was recently released this year after being in prison for 10 years for selling crack and cocaine. He currently lives with his girlfriend a few blocks away from Betsy's house. He visits Jermaine and his other children a few times a month, but Jermaine reports that he does not get along with his father very well and "does not really know him." Jermaine's mother raised him and his sisters until 3 years ago when she was placed in prison for 2 years for selling drugs. She was also released this past year but lives 2 hours away in another city working as a waitress and going to school. Jermaine has seen his mother only once since she was released from prison; however, he talks to her frequently on the phone and reports feeling close to his mom.

Since living with his grandmother, Jermaine has become involved in a local gang. This gang is well known for violence, drugs, and other negative behaviors, such as stealing and dropping out of school. In the past month Jermaine was picked up for illegal operation of a vehicle and possession of marijuana. Jermaine was placed in a juvenile correctional facility for approximately 6 months. In this facility, he is mandated to receive individual and family counseling, specifically focusing on drug and alcohol use. The goal of the court is for Jermaine to stop using alcohol and drugs.

At intake, Jermaine claimed that he did not have a drug or alcohol problem. When asked to clarify his statement, he reported that he did not use any of the substances, "besides drinking every now and then." When asked about the marijuana the police found in his car, he reported that he "did not use drugs;

he just sold them." Selling drugs was not noted in the police report or the court mandate to counseling. Although Jermaine reported that he did not have an alcohol or drug problem, he scored fairly high on the Substance Abuse Subtle Screening Inventory–Adolescent 2 (SASSI-A2) that he was asked to take when he was brought into the correctional facility.

It has been difficult to get family sessions with his grandmother Betsy, his legal guardian, because she is legally blind and has to find someone to drive her to the scheduled sessions. During the three family sessions you have been able to have with Betsy and Jermaine in the 4 months he has been in the facility, she consistently reports that she "loves Jermaine and just wants him back home." In the most recent session, 2 weeks ago, when she was asked about rules, discipline, or other activities that go on in the home, Betsy says that she does not need to discipline Jermaine because he is a "good kid," and she does not want to scold him because she wants him to be able to tell her anything. She believes that by punishing Jermaine she will create a situation or environment that he will not be honest with her and come to her when he is having a problem. When you have confronted her about the fact that Jermaine has not told her that he has skipped school in the past or that he sells drugs, Betsy just shrugs her shoulders, looks at Jermaine and asks him, "Are you going to lie to me about that again?" Jermaine looked at the floor and said, "No." Betsy tells you that she is satisfied with that answer and sees no reason to change the way she disciplines Jermaine.

Incident

Jermaine has been in the facility for approximately 4 months and the courts have already begun to process his release date, which is scheduled for 2 weeks from today. Recently, Jermaine has been less vocal in groups, among his peers, and to facility staff. You know that Jermaine was given a weekend pass from the correctional facility to go home on a home visit this past weekend. When you bring up the topic of his recent behavior in the correctional facility in this individual counseling session, he does not say much to you at first. Once you bring up the topic of his home visit and his grandmother, Jermaine looks at the floor. Through previous conversations, you know that Jermaine holds his grandmother in high respect and continually has told you that he does not want to do anything that will hurt his grandmother or that will cause him to lose her respect.

After asking Jermaine probing questions, he informs you that he has always held his family in high esteem because they have never "used drugs; they have just sold them." Both of his parents have sold drugs, and Jermaine informs you that he has been selling marijuana, crack, and cocaine for the past year. He started selling drugs to buy "nice things" that he normally could not afford, as well as to help his grandmother pay the utility bills and buy groceries. Jermaine informs you that if he did not sell drugs, there would be no food on the table for his family since his grandmother has been unable to work in the past 10 years because of her disability. He reports being upset because during the

Critical Incidents in Addictions Counseling

home visit, he found out that his grandmother has been using his crack supply and has been since he began selling. He reports that he does not know what to think because "his family doesn't use drugs; they are not that stupid."

Discussion

After the session, you call Jermaine's probation officer to inform her of what was going on in the house with Jermaine's grandmother, as well as Jermaine's selling drugs to support the family. The probation officer reports that she has been in the house and has not seen any drug activity; thus, she does not see a problem with releasing him to the custody of his grandmother.

Questions

1. What is your responsibility, as the counselor, at this point regarding the new information provided to you about his grandmother's drug use and Jermaine's selling drugs to support his family? Does this new information impact the safety of the client returning home?
2. What information do you provide to the court, if any? The original court mandate mentioned nothing of selling drugs or of other drug use in the home. Do you release this information, or would this be considered breaking confidentiality since this was not the original goal of the court?
3. Would you recommend that Jermaine stay in the facility longer, be placed in another home, be released to his grandmother, or an alternative option?
4. What additional interventions might you use given that Jermaine's SASSI-A2 scores indicate he has a substance abuse problem, but he still has not admitted to using alcohol or drugs?
5. Involving probation or parole officers tends to be an integral aspect of working with court-mandated clients; however, what is a counselor's responsibility for the safety of his or her client when the probation officer does not have the same opinion or accept the client's self-reported information?

■Response

Todd F. Lewis

Jermaine's case is a good representation of common issues surrounding clients who are court mandated to attend counseling. I first want to commend this counselor for being highly aware of the multitude of issues surrounding this case. It appears that the counselor appropriately used clarification, probing, assessment (SASSI-A), and confrontation. It also seems that some attempt at family counseling has ensued, with mixed results. Aside from seemingly difficult decisions this counselor must make regarding Jermaine's counseling, there also are several legal and ethical issues involved, particularly surrounding information recently divulged.

Considering the additional information that Jermaine revealed, the counselor is placed in a quandary regarding issues such as confidentiality and privileged communication. The counselor would not be obligated to provide any information to the court unless specifically requested to do so. However, the counselor should be prepared to provide information that addresses the original court mandate, as this would likely be requested. If this facility is a federally funded substance abuse program, a general rule of thumb is that confidentiality must be maintained in nearly all aspects of counseling (McWhirter, McWhirter, McWhirter, & McWhirter, 2004), unless it was determined that the client was in danger or likely to hurt someone else. With this in mind, then, the counselor would need to assess whether the grandmother's substance use represents a "clear and imminent danger" to Jermaine or others. If so, this information would need to be reported to the proper authorities, and the counselor would be wise to document the reasons for sharing this information.

Without the court mandating Jermaine to continue in the facility (it seems from the case that the courts are already processing his release), the counselor cannot force Jermaine into further treatment. However, if the release date is contingent on the counselor's final assessment related to the original court mandate, then the counselor may be in a position to influence further counseling for Jermaine. An additional question the counselor must ask is, "Can Jermaine continue to benefit from being in this facility, or would another alternative be appropriate?" I am supportive of providing clients a "menu" of treatment options, if possible. Because Jermaine's time at the facility is winding down, it would be important to assess the degree of change made, the appropriateness of returning home, and additional counseling options. Part of my approach would be to elicit from Jermaine his thoughts, feelings, and concerns about each option. I would continually encourage him to be as involved in his own counseling as possible, assess resistance and motivation, and ensure that rapport between us stays strong.

Question 4 seems to tap into a key issue surrounding any concept of change: motivation. From this question, it can be assumed that for most of Jermaine's tenure in the facility he has remained in the *precontemplative* stage of change, characterized by clients who are not yet considering change or who are unwilling or unable to change. Often, clients who present as precontemplative will not be amenable to most therapeutic interventions, because these usually assume a person is ready to make significant improvements in one's life. As a general rule, overly confrontational methods should be avoided with such clients. Rather than "breaking down" resistance, such interventions seem to have the paradoxical effect of increasing resistance.

Given this state of affairs, I would encourage the counselor to try a *motivational interviewing* approach with Jermaine (e.g., Miller & Rollnick, 1991; Miller, Rollnick, & Moyers, 1998). The goals of this approach would be to lower levels of resistance, increase intrinsic motivation to change, and resolve

Critical Incidents in Addictions Counseling

Jermaine's ambivalence about substance use. Establishing rapport and building trust are crucial elements for someone who is precontemplative. Adopting a counseling posture that honors the client's story and is empathetic to the struggles he or she faces is at the heart of a motivational philosophy.

Motivational strategies for someone who is precontemplative begin with raising doubts or concerns in the client about substance-using patterns. For example, you might explore the meaning of the events that brought Jermaine to treatment, elicit his perception of the problem, offer factual information about the risks of substance use, and provide personalized feedback regarding his assessment results. This last suggestion specifically addresses Jermaine's assessment findings according to the SASSI-A.

Providing personalized feedback can be a powerful force in motivating change (Miller & Rollnick, 1991). I liken this to receiving feedback from a physician that one's cholesterol is too high. On hearing this feedback, one's own internal sources of motivation are mobilized, and one will start paying attention to diet and exercise. The same may be true in this case. On learning of the assessment results, Jermaine may begin the process of examining his own behavior, which may spark his own internal motivations to consider changing. As Miller and Rollnick (1991) noted, however, "it's not just the words but the music." That is, *how* you provide the feedback can be just as (or perhaps more) important than the actual content in helping people to change. Thus, from a motivational interviewing perspective, the counselor would avoid saying something like, "Well, Jermaine, clearly from these results you are in serious trouble with substance use. It looks like you are becoming an addict and you should be really concerned." This statement engenders resistance because it conveys disrespect by telling the client how he should feel, a view that implies the counselor is the "all-knowing" expert on the client. Additionally, the use of labels (such as the word *addict*) is a sure way to harden resistance toward changing behavior. Instead, an approach to feedback such as the following might be more appropriate:

> As you can see here, Jermaine, this [section of the test] demonstrates where you lie compared with other individuals your age. I don't know whether this will matter to you or not, but according to these results, you are at the 95th percentile of those similar to you in age who drink. This means that you tend to consume more alcohol than 95% of your peers. As I give you this information, what are you thinking at this point?

The last question is designed to elicit the client's own concerns, thoughts, and feelings on the feedback provided. Notice, too, that this example does not resort to a "scare tactic" tone; rather, it conveys respect for the client and implies that the counselor is interested in what sense the client makes of the information. At the end of providing the feedback from the SASSI-A, I recommend that the counselor (a) summarize the risks and problems that emerged from the assessment, (b) summarize Jermaine's own reactions to the feedback, *including statements that acknowledge a need for change*, and (c) offer Jermaine an invitation to add to or correct the summary (Miller & Rollnick, 1991).

Forming and keeping positive relationships with parole or probation officers is an important part of any counselor working with youths. In this case, there appears to be a discrepancy between what the counselor and probation officer believe and information provided by Jermaine. It is important to keep in mind that the counselor's job is to provide counseling services to Jermaine and inform the proper authorities if he is in danger of being hurt or hurting self or others. Assuming there was perceived risk in Jermaine's comments, the counselor took reasonable and appropriate actions to inform the probation officer of the additional information. I would encourage the counselor to follow up with the probation officer and reinforce his or her concern for what Jermaine revealed. If the probation officer is still in disagreement, the counselor might consider speaking to the probation officer's superior or inviting him or her to a treatment team meeting, in which concerns from other individuals can be voiced, discussed, and processed. The important issue for the counselor, however, is to take responsible and reasonable actions to ensure the safety of the client. Unfortunately, it is impossible for counselors to be with clients 24 hours a day to ensure their safety. However, what counselors can do is be vigilant, consult with colleagues, and take reasonable steps to report and document actions. From a legal standpoint, awareness and action, not infallibility, are expected (Vacc & Loesch, 2000).

■References

McWhirter, J. J., McWhirter, B. T., McWhirter, A. M., & McWhirter, E. H. (2004). *At-risk youth: A comprehensive response* (3rd ed.). Pacific Grove, CA: Brooks/Cole.

Miller, W. R., & Rollnick, S. (1991). *Motivational interviewing: Preparing people to change addictive behavior*. New York: Guilford Press.

Miller, W. R., Rollnick, S., & Moyers, T. B. (Director). (1998). *Motivational interviewing: Professional training series 1998* [Film series]. (Available from UNM/CASAA, 260 Yale SE, Albuquerque, NM 87106)

Vacc, N. A., & Loesch, L. C. (2000). *Professional orientation to counseling* (3rd ed.). Philadelphia: Brunner-Routledge.

16

Addictions Counseling With Adolescents

■Critical Incident

Gerald A. Juhnke

Background

Sixteen-year-old Rashad was an African American male who lived with his 24-year-old custodial sister, Amber, and her 27-year-old partner, Andrew. Rashad's father had left the family when Rashad was 10 years old. Between the time of their father's leaving and Amber's moving out of the family's trailer 2 years earlier, Rashad and Amber had been nearly "inseparable." Their mother had a history of chronic cocaine and heroine substance dependence with substance-related arrests (e.g., possession of cocaine with intent to deliver, prostitution). Within the previous 2-year period, their mother's advanced Alzheimer's disease resulted in an assisted-care facility placement. Rashad originally attempted to live independently in his mother's trailer without adult supervision. However, just 3 weeks later, Rashad was arrested on multiple charges. These included larceny, possession of a controlled substance, and assault charges. Because of his nonmajority age, Child Protective Services became involved. A juvenile court magistrate gave Rashad and his sister two choices. Rashad could either become a minor ward of the state—initially serving his time at a juvenile detention center and then moving into a foster care facility—or Amber, his sister, could assume legal guardianship for Rashad. Additionally, Amber's legal guardianship required Rashad to (a) live in Amber's trailer, (b) participate in two random drug screens each month, (c) attend school and pass courses, and (d) participate in weekly counseling sessions for a period no less than 30 weeks. After significant debate, Rashad and Amber agreed to Amber's guardianship and Rashad moved into Amber's trailer.

Prior to Rashad's initial counseling appointment, he completed the Minnesota Multiphasic Personality Inventory–Adolescent (MMPI-A) and the Substance Abuse Subtle Screening Inventory–Adolescent (SASSI-A). Assessment results suggested that Rashad likely qualified for conduct disorder and an undetermined alcohol or other drug (AOD) dependence diagnosis. It was noted within the clinical interview that Rashad regularly used phencyclidine (PCP) and met the established criteria for PCP dependence. Furthermore, via the MMPI-A and the clinical interview, it was noted that Rashad (a) perceived significant familial discord within his current home, (b) had difficulties with authority figures, (c) was hypersensitive to criticism, and (d) had conduct and behavior problems. Amber, who indicated in a separate interview that she (and her live-in partner, Andrew, later substantiated these concerns) and Rashad were "constantly arguing with one another." Amber reported that Rashad would not follow "house rules." Amber further indicated that Rashad had instigated several physical "shoving episodes" and was verbally abusive to Amber and Andrew.

Incident

A hospital social worker and Rashad's Child Protective Services case manager referred Rashad. Twice within the preceding 14 days, Rashad had intentionally burned himself with lighter fluid. This resulted in second-degree burns to his face and neck.

During our first counseling session Rashad and Amber helped me develop a 14-day behavioral baseline of Rashad's AOD-abusing and self-injurious behaviors. The targeted behaviors occurred primarily on Friday and Saturday evenings when Amber and Andrew's friends were "partying at the trailer." Rashad would become violent when Amber, Andrew, and their guests were intoxicated and the party was about to come to end. It was at these times Rashad would use PCP. Amber believed Rashad's PCP use caused his violent behaviors. Rashad denied PCP use as the precipitator and indicated he became violent when "people insulted me."

A reverse behavioral baseline was drawn below the targeted baseline. It was noted that Rashad had not demonstrated targeted behaviors (a) when Rashad and others were not consuming alcohol or PCP and (b) during daytime and or weekday evenings. Both baselines provided contingency contract criteria.

Rashad and Amber jointly created a contingency contract. Rashad agreed to (a) clean his room on Mondays and Thursdays before 5 p.m.; (b) be home no later than 11 p.m.; (c) remain PCP and AOD abstinent; (d) attend a young people's 12-step meeting on Friday and Saturday evenings; (e) be verbally pleasant and nonabusive toward Amber, Andrew, and their guests; (e) not fight; and (f) not be self-injurious. In return, Amber would allow Rashad the privilege of staying in her trailer and included specifically outlined television and food privileges. Furthermore, Amber indicated she would file a police report and have Rashad removed from the trailer upon any noted infraction.

The assessment and initial intervention took an entire afternoon. Rashad indicated he wished to stay in Amber's trailer, especially with her cable television and her ample food supply. Amber and Rashad agreed to return the following day for another session. Amber also agreed to ask Andrew to attend the next day's scheduled meeting.

Cost-Benefit Analysis Interventions

Rashad, Amber, and Andrew arrived the next day as scheduled and were informed that Rashad's juvenile probation officer and Child Protective Services case manager wished to join the session. The session began once the necessary releases were signed. We started by thanking Andrew for his attendance and recognizing Rashad's contingency contract compliance. Rashad's probation officer and case manager then summarized Rashad's options related to drug screens and housing. Noncompliance would result in immediate removal from Amber's trailer.

After Rashad's probation officer and case manger left, a cost-benefit analysis was introduced. Here, Rashad identified violent, AOD-abusing, and self-injurious behavior benefits. The benefits included (a) gaining attention, (b) escaping boredom, and (c) gaining nurturing behaviors. Rashad admitted a number of target behavior costs. These included others' verbalized feelings of anger and disappointment, loss of friends, mandated counseling, and pending detention time.

Costs associated with eliminating targeted behaviors were also discussed. Rashad reported that he was concerned if he was not violent that he would be perceived as "weak." Additionally, he reported costs related to losing peer relationships—"When I'm using [PCP] everybody wants to be my friend." Costs associated with eliminating his self-injurious behaviors included losing Amber's support and being held accountable by his probation officer. The primary reported benefit for changing his targeted behaviors was "staying free from foster care." He noted that he did not want to leave Amber's trailer, because "it's one easy life."

Amber reported the costs associated with removing Rashad from the trailer included losing others' perceptions she was "self-sacrificing" and her fear of losing "my last family contact." Andrew indicated that Rashad's violent and addicted behaviors potentially benefited him as Amber relied more heavily on Andrew when she was "stressed out by Rashad."

Discussion

Rashad, Amber, and Andrew noted insight and behavioral changes resulting from behavioral and reverse behavioral baselines and the cost-benefits analysis. Specifically, Rashad indicated that being removed from the trailer with its cable television and available food far outweighed any potential benefits of using PCP or alcohol, or acting violently toward self or others. Additionally, we were able to identify new behaviors that Rashad, Amber, and Andrew could implement when Rashad felt "bored" or needed others' attention, support, or nurturance.

Amber and Andrew also reported gaining insight as to why they were not holding Rashad accountable for his addicted and violent behaviors. They made a contract with each other outlining how they would respond should Rashad not follow "house rules."

Questions

1. Although I believe the symbiotic relationships between Rashad, Amber, and Andrew were in part instigating and continuing Rashad's PCP use and his self-injurious and violent behaviors, other professionals with whom I have discussed the case believe using a systemic intervention such as this could entrap Amber and Andrew in parenting Rashad—potentially doing harm to Amber and Andrew. What types of counseling interventions might you have used instead of or in conjunction with this behavioral systemic intervention? Specifically, I am wondering if you would believe couples counseling might be appropriate for Amber and Andrew.
2. Given the nature of addictions and the effects of PCP on behaviors, what additional interventions might you have used individually with Rashad?
3. I have found that involving probation officers and case managers in initial counseling sessions helpful. However, I also do not want clients to perceive that I am part of the judicial system. What ideas might you suggest to ensure clients understand they are doing counseling with me and that I am separate from those who are mandating their treatment?
4. Also, besides gaining releases from clients authorizing me to share information with probation officers and case mangers, are there other confidentiality issues I may need to address in cases such as this?

■Response

Virginia A. Kelly

Certainly, the counselor in the described case displays a level of professionalism and knowledge base that is commendable and ultimately helpful to this adolescent client. The use of behavioral systemic counseling interventions with Rashad proved successful in the short term and may have resulted in offsetting consequences that were potentially devastating and life altering for the client. For example, the possibility of placement into a facility where Rashad may have ultimately gotten "lost in the system" was a very real possibility in the described case.

In addition to the utilization of clinically astute assessment and intervention strategies, the counselor poses relevant questions and conveys openness to the consideration of alternative or additional methods of treatment that may enhance outcomes with Rashad.

In Question 1, the counselor appears to be assessing the possibility of integrating strategies that may find their basis in family/systems theory. This presents possibilities that may result in the incorporation of less behaviorally focused strategies along with the behavioral interventions already described. This particular question is paramount, as we know that addiction is a family issue. As such, every family member should participate in treatment. Specifically, in the described case, I cannot help but wonder about the precise nature of Amber and Andrew's substance use. In the event that they too are struggling in this area, it might in fact prove futile to treat Rashad exclusively.

In addition to assessing and possibly treating Amber and Andrew, it may be useful to consider the role of the symbiotic relationships described and discuss possible systemic approaches to avoid their destructive influence in future family interactions, and to investigate the ways in which they may be supporting addictive behavior within the family system. Given the intense nature of Rashad's family background, the formation of such a symbiotic relationship between Rashad and his sister makes sense on a clinical level. In addition, the inclusion of Amber's partner, Andrew, into the mix has the potential of destabilizing the system in additional ways. The use of couples counseling initially, and family counseling ultimately, may serve to defuse the intensity of the relationships described and provide a forum in which to learn and practice alternative ways of interacting and establishing and maintaining appropriate and useful boundaries within the family system.

I might begin this process by assessing Amber and Andrew's current level of satisfaction with the family dynamics. This might include specific questions related to how they perceive their current roles within the family and where they might desire change. My goal might be to gain a clear sense of current functioning within the family. Depending on the issues presented, I might attempt to integrate interventions based on a structural approach that would allow for the alterations of boundaries within the family system as well as that of the subsystems currently operating within the system.

In response to Question 2, let me first state that PCP is certainly a scary substance. The use of PCP is associated with erratic and unpredictable behavior that can include violent episodes. With this in mind, it seems that this is not a situation that can be taken lightly or avoided on any level. In addition to regular testing and the clear understanding of the consequences for a positive result, it seems that Amber and Andrew must become "experts" on the use and abuse of PCP. If either adult suspects use, they must feel free to contact authorities (i.e., the police or local emergency room) quickly in the event that behavior escalates at a rate that eliminates the possibility of conducting a drug test. In addition, it seems that Amber and Andrew must consider that Rashad is likely to experiment with and ultimately abuse alternative substances as well. What we know is that adolescents rarely use a single substance. The likelihood that other substances may enter the picture should be openly discussed and expected. Finally, given the nature of addiction and what we currently know regarding successful treatment, it may benefit Amber and Andrew to attend a local Al-Anon meeting. Specifically, if they are able to find a meeting for parents of addicts, they will be able to access the support of individuals currently experiencing struggles similar to their own. The use of the 12-step model in managing the disease of addiction continues to provide a model and structure for continued recovery within the entire family system that has not been met by the use of any other single model (Substance Abuse and Mental Health Services Administration and Department of Veterans Affairs, 2003).

In response to Question 3, I believe that the counselor is absolutely "doing the right thing" when she or he introduces the probation officer into the counseling process at the time indicated in the described case. It is hoped that in the time that has elapsed prior to the introduction of the criminal justice system into the process, the counselor has been able to develop a basis of trust and rapport with Rashad. In this case, the counselor can rely on this relationship. I believe that the counselor must anticipate anger on the part of Rashad at the introduction of the probation officer. In addition, the counselor should anticipate manipulation on the part of Rashad that is likely to include the use of inducing guilt and blame. These are the hallmarks of addictive behavior. However, this should not dictate the course of treatment. If the counselor believes that there is a real risk of Rashad using alcohol or other drugs, and thus violating the contract, the introduction of the probation officer may serve to prohibit behavior that might otherwise lead to consequences that will harm Rashad in far more critical ways than divulging a confidence. The counselor may liken this experience to that of a parent who makes a decision in the best interest of a child when the parent knows that the child may resent the parent temporarily. The parent may be counting on a long-term effect whereby the child will eventually understand the reason for the parent's original decision.

Finally, in response to Question 4, the only other group I may want to access in the described case is that of Rashad's school community. If Rashad is attending school on a regular basis, he is spending a great deal of time with the individuals within that community. I may desire to develop a contact at the school that I can check in with regarding his behavior there. I would most likely seek permission to contact Rashad's school counselor in an effort to develop a connection with an individual who can monitor Rashad in that environment and perhaps intervene where I do not have access.

In conclusion, I would like to reiterate that I believe the counselor in this case has done a very thorough and commendable job. The described case involves circumstances that create great complication and myriad issues that have the potential of affecting Rashad's treatment. Unfortunately, it is a case that is presented often within the addictions field and illustrates the overwhelming nature of treatment for these clients.

■Reference

Substance Abuse and Mental Health Services Administration and Department of Veterans Affairs. (2003). *Self-help organizations for alcohol and drug problems: Towards evidence-based practice and policy—Workgroup on substance abuse self-help organizations*. Retrieved August 16, 2003, from www.chce.research.med.va.gov/chce/pdfs/Vasama_feb1103.pdf

17 Gambling Addictions

■Critical Incident

David Lundberg and Virginia A. Kelly

Background

Mike was a 46-year-old Caucasian engineering technician from the southwestern United States who relocated to Las Vegas to maintain employment. He had been married for 17 years to Audrey and had two children, 16-year-old Shannon and 14-year-old Derrick. Mike always enjoyed gambling, and this had been an ongoing source of stress and conflict within his marriage. Audrey had felt for years that Mike was out of control with his gambling, while Mike maintained that this was not the case.

Incident

Mike was referred to me for counseling after being arrested and charged with embezzlement. Mike's boss discovered that he had been stealing from the company for many months and turned him in to the authorities. During his trial, Mike disclosed that he had stolen the money to pay off gambling debts and maintain access to the local casinos. As it turned out, Mike was going to the casinos an average of four to five times per week. It was discovered that he would frequently stay all night, never going home or contacting his wife. Mike was eventually charged and found guilty of fraud and embezzlement. Because this was Mike's first offense, he was able to negotiate a reduced sentence in return for agreeing to participate in treatment for his gambling addiction.

By the time I met with Mike for our first counseling session, he was in financial ruins, his marriage had failed, and he had a strained (at best) relationship with his children, whom he saw only intermittently. Despite the state of his life, Mike was still very much in denial regarding his gambling addiction. He reported that he did not have a real problem with gambling; he simply liked to go to the casinos occasionally. He stated, "My real problems were my marriage and my job. My wife was always on my back and my boss never did pay me a decent wage."

During the initial stages of counseling, my primary goal was related to breaking through Mike's denial to move him to a place where he could begin to consider a commitment to the recovery process. I was fairly directive in my approach during this phase of the counseling process and used a predominantly cognitive approach. I asked Mike to tell me about some of the gambling addicts he knew and attempted to weave in a sense of where he might stand in comparison with them. I also focused heavily on Mike's relationship with his children, as this was his greatest source of pain. Finally, I referred Mike to a Gamblers Anonymous group that was run out of our agency.

As Mike became more committed to attending group counseling and grew more decisive in his desire to heal his relationships with his children, he began to make marked progress. He seemed to break through the denial and began to address some core issues. However, Mike did remain focused on "blaming his wife" and was not assuming full responsibility for his addiction. Although progress had been made, Mike continued to relapse from time to time, always citing his wife as his trigger.

Discussion

Although Mike did make progress in his treatment, he was not able to stabilize his financial situation and continued to occasionally relapse. He was able to reconnect with his children. However, owing to his lack of commitment to his recovery and his unstable financial situation, visitations were inconsistent and frequently supervised. As soon as Mike had met his legal obligation to treatment, he stopped attending both sessions and Gamblers Anonymous meetings.

Questions

1. What other intervention or strategies might have been used to assist Mike in breaking through his denial?
2. What, if any, role should the family have played in Mike's treatment?
3. Were there alternative strategies that might have been used to keep Mike in treatment?
4. What was the counselor's obligation in terms of follow-up with Mike, given the nature of his referral and treatment?

▌Response

Robin Guill Liles

Incident Treatment Review

Both scientific research and clinical observation suggest that regardless of addiction etiology the first step in the recovery process is personal acceptance of addiction. Thus, the counselor's initial counseling goal to help Mike move from disowning to accepting responsibility for his gambling behaviors fits with addiction counseling good practices. It is not unusual for people in addiction-related life crises (e.g., failed marriages, legal difficulties) to experience intensely negative feelings such as despondency, helplessness, even hopelessness. Accordingly, the counselor appears to make another sound clinical decision to implement a cognitive approach to therapy. In other words, given Mike's professional background and presumed education level, working from a cognitive stance would encourage Mike to "step back" from any overwhelming emotions, view his internal and external life turmoil in a rational manner, and through cognitive restructuring, use his intellectual abilities in a positive way.

Asking Mike to consider other gambling addicts whom he knew, and to describe ways in which he believed he was both similar and dissimilar to them, could provide helpful assessment information. Addiction specialists understand that people who are ambivalent about their recovery often view themselves as able to "control" their addictions and that this special ability clearly sets them apart from the "typical addict." By contrast, addicted individuals who are fully committed to their recovery tend to see themselves as personally responsible for, and vulnerable to, the negative consequences of their behaviors.

The counselor states that Mike's commitment to heal relationships with his children and to build supportive relationships with Gamblers Anonymous members appeared to contribute to his progress. Helping Mike focus on his strained relationships with his children may have been the counselor's most powerful intervention. Existentially, Mike's personal anxiety related to his children probably kindled, and could continue to nourish, his desire to implement important life changes, thus potentially upgrading his relationships with his children and reducing his internal discomfort. Finally, encouraging Mike to attend Gamblers Anonymous seems reasonable. Participation in a 12-step group may provide Mike with the opportunity to connect with others who are struggling to live with a gambling addiction.

On the other hand, the counselor also reports that whereas Mike made "marked progress," he failed to cross the recovery threshold, whereby he no longer experienced any negative sequelae associated with his addiction. The counselor further states that Mike continued to "blame his wife" for his addiction, identifying her as the "trigger" for his gambling relapses.

Other Confounding Factors

In reviewing Mike's treatment, it could be helpful to discuss other factors possibly confounding his full recovery. Current reports indicate that whereas gambling addiction is similar to other addictions such as alcohol and other drug (AOD) use, the nature of gambling addiction also appears somewhat different. For instance, behaviorists would view gambling as a conditioned response intermittently reinforced through occasional "wins." Such reinforcement has been historically recognized as a powerful influence in strengthening and sustaining behavioral activity (Ferster, 1958). In other words, whereas AOD addictions are universally deemed problematic, an unexpected "financial windfall," infusing conceivably much-needed dollars into an individual's or family's budget, may be simultaneously regarded as a blessing and a problem. This conflicted emotional response to winning is likely to be felt by both the gambling person and those connected to him or her. If so, then gambling's intermittently reinforcing properties are enhanced and could foil Mike's recovery efforts.

Potenza et al. (2003) provided preliminary data ($N = 21$) indicating pathological gamblers who view videotapes of gambling scenarios exhibit decreased neural activity in areas of the brain thought to regulate impulsive behavior. These data are intriguing and may inform future intervention opportunities. However, gambling addiction, unlike AOD addiction, cannot readily be indexed through observable, physical symptoms (e.g., intoxication). Accordingly, gambling addiction may be more easily hidden from public view. In fact, recent efforts to measure the reliability of gamblers' self-reported gambling behaviors through gambler and collateral (e.g., spouse, friend) concordance assessment interviews produced mediocre agreement results (intraclass correlation coefficients ranging from .46 to .65; Hodgins & Makarchuk, 2003). Thus, pragmatically speaking, the potential for the gambling person to act deceptively regarding his or her gambling behaviors could neutralize the promise of any counseling benefits afforded by supportive others (e.g., spouse, friend). In the case of Mike, it may be useful to wonder about trust and accountability issues and how they could be presently affecting his personal relationships.

From a societal point of view, legalized gambling appears to have a strong foothold in the United States. In the past, legal gambling was for the most part geographically confined, and in order to legally gamble, individuals were obliged to overcome certain logistical restrictions. However, the Associated Press (2004) reported that today some variety of legalized gambling exists in every U.S. state except Utah. Community leaders and developers often endorse gambling hotels and casinos as vehicles for boosting local economies. Thirty-nine U.S. states have legalized lotteries to bolster floundering state budgets; among those states that do not have legal lotteries, consideration to put a lottery into effect is ongoing. Relatedly, Gehring (1999) proposed that many individuals purchasing lottery tickets may be responding to mixed media messages. On the one hand, groups who defend state lotteries often claim that revenues will be used to support the greater social good (e.g., education) and that anyone purchasing lottery tickets is in effect "making an investment" in the community's or state's future. By contrast, advertising language designed to encourage lottery ticket purchases may nudge people toward the belief that there is a causal albeit lucky relationship between a lottery-ticket purchase and a big win. For instance, one New York campaign advertisement read, "You Can't Win If You Don't Play"; and in Maryland, a similar advertisement stated, "Play Today. Cash Tonight." Perhaps the newest and most troubling gambling frontier is the Internet. A quick Google search using key words *gambling* and *online* essentially produces an unlimited number of related Web sites. To date, legislative attempts to make online gambling illegal have failed; thus, regardless of the person's age, current access to gambling opportunities is as easy as a "mouse click" away. Finally, relevant statistics suggest that sometime in their lifetime between 2.5 and 3.2 million American adults meet *Diagnostic and Statistical Manual of Mental Disorders* (4th ed., Text Revision [*DSM-IV-TR*]; American Psychiatric Association, 2000) criteria for pathological gambling, and that in any given year, between 1.7 and 2.6 million Americans meet the criteria. Perhaps most worrisome are prevalence rates describing adolescent pathological gambling. Reports indicate that 1.1 million teenagers between 12 and 18 years old currently meet diagnostic criteria for pathological gambling (National Gambling Impact Study Commission, 1999). Thus, American society appears accepting of gambling activities, and implicit to this acceptance may be an emerging sense of social, political, and even moral gambling legitimacy. If this is the case, then it is reasonable to assume that Mike's recovery process will be further hampered by gambling's ubiquitous nature.

Finally, conventional wisdom suggests that job loss and unemployment are associated with feelings of personal loss and purposelessness, and together these issues pose particular mood, anxiety, and adjustment challenges. It is unclear whether Mike has been able to find another job. However, it is logical to think that with his employment and legal history, Mike's ability to secure a job, with the status and prestige equivalent to that of his previous job, is limited. Thus, Mike's already upsetting life situation may be further exacerbated.

Other Interventions and Strategies Addressing Mike's Denial

In thinking about other interventions or strategies useful in assisting Mike in breaking through his denial, it could be helpful to implement reality-based discussions intended to offset or minimize the powerful properties of intermittent positive reinforcement. The counselor states that he or she utilized a cognitive and "fairly directive" approach to therapy. The value of this approach has already been highlighted. However, gambling activities largely encompass a set of negative behaviors with related consequences. Mike needs to notice that whereas gambling behaviors may unexpectedly bring about financial windfalls, and that these windfalls may be initially viewed as much needed and well timed, the benefits are impermanent, and the long-term temporal, psychological, and emotional costs are too great. Thus, in addition to cognitive interventions, it could be useful to add behavioral and emotional components, systematically using a cost-benefit analysis. With cost-benefit analysis, the client is asked to identify and describe the benefits he or she derives from negative behaviors, and the potential costs associated with these benefits (Gerald A. Juhnke, personal communication, June 2000). It is hoped that the analysis then shapes the client's present and future decision making in a positive direction.

Control-based reality theory (Glasser, 1997) suggests that human beings have five basic needs, including survival, love, power, freedom, and fun, and that all behaviors are purposeful, intended to satisfy these needs. Hence, working from a cost-benefit perspective, the counselor might hypothesize that one benefit Mike gains from gambling relapses is the chance to recoup past financial losses and overcome current financial stressors (i.e., survival). Another hypothesized gambling benefit may be that when Mike finds himself in a gaming venue, among gaming employees, he feels understood, accepted, appreciated, and perhaps even loved. A third hypothesis could suggest Mike's addictive impulses all too easily translate into feelings of personal power and freedom. Finally, the counselor may hypothesize that Mike continues to relapse because gambling is simply great fun, bringing Mike unmatched personal enjoyment.

Carrying Glasser's (1997) theoretical perspective forward through cost-benefit analysis, the counselor would "check in" with Mike to ascertain the validity of his or her hypotheses. Mike may (or may not) agree that gambling relapses are largely financially motivated and that his hope is to recoup losses and overcome current financial stress. Nonetheless, the counselor should launch discussions targeting the role employment plays in successful adult living. Mike needs to understand that beyond drawing income, experiencing vocational purpose, regardless of employment prestige or status, is psychologically and emotionally important. The counselor could bolster these conversations with data describing the probability of accumulating wealth through lucky gaming and serendipity versus steady work and thriftiness. The counselor might have Mike calculate total dollar winnings and total losses, including legal costs and related financial penalties, and then make win/loss comparisons. Additionally, using the total losses figure, lost interest income relative to gambling years could be computed. These and other simple mathematical calculations establish incontrovertible evidence indicating that gambling is a poor, if not outright disastrous, financial decision. It also should be noted that whereas in this case the counseling relationship's nature is not necessarily defined as career oriented, career counseling is historical to the counseling profession and may offer Mike real help.

Given his employment and legal problems, it is possible Mike is experiencing shameful feelings and senses rejection from family, friends, and working colleagues. Thus, discussions surrounding gambling's pervasive, apparently inescapable, and perhaps "triggering" societal presence are germane to Mike's recovery. In other words, if Mike admits that gaming venues are places where he experiences feelings of warmth, understanding, acceptance, and perhaps even love, then the counselor could ask Mike to consider costs related to "feeling at home" in gaming venues. In the most therapeutic sense, Mike would be able and willing to identify and describe these costs. However, if the counselor discerns that Mike is either reluctant or unable to move in this direction, then he or she may want to pose some possibilities. For example, the counselor could wonder out loud about the truly caring nature of people whose livelihood depends exclusively on other people losing money. Or the counselor may speculate about the level of support gaming owners provide when their customers get into financial and legal trouble. Another tack could include canvassing Mike's thoughts about whether or not gambling personnel could adequately support and care for those whom Mike loves, such as his children. By contrast, if Mike repudiates the counselor's hypothesis, claiming no personal relationship to gaming

Critical Incidents in Addictions Counseling

venues, owners, and employees, then the counselor might ask Mike to describe places where he finds haven and refuge, as well as the relationships in his life that foster nurturance and love. Gently nudging Mike to talk about ways in which gambling may have separated him from these places and loved ones could be helpful. Again, the greatest therapeutic advances would probably derive from Mike's ability to experience self-awareness and insight, and the counselor should facilitate this process through respectful dialogue and sensitive questioning. Finally, the counselor may want to consider concluding this counseling segment on an existential note, referencing all humanity's basic need to love and be loved.

Recent research suggests pathological gamblers suffer a reduction in brain activity thought to regulate impulsive behaviors (Potenza et al., 2003). If these preliminary data prove conclusive, then discussions surrounding the third and fourth hypotheses (i.e., Mike experiences feelings of power, freedom, and fun when gambling) may be deemed particularly important to the counseling process. In other words, given the circumstances, it seems likely that Mike would validate these hypotheses, perhaps describing actual time spent gambling as exciting and thrilling, regardless of his win/loss position. Moreover, from a cost-benefit point of view, the pleasant sensations Mike associates with gambling, including elevated mood and reduced anxiety, together with his fundamental human desire for power, freedom, and fun, could translate into overwhelming benefits, with very little if any perceived cost or downside.

Yet, experimental behaviorists have established that addicted and unremitting pleasure-seeking behaviors evolve in a negative and unhealthy direction, potentially including self-injurious activity (Ferster, 1958). Helping Mike define and internalize gambling costs related to power, freedom, and fun is necessary; otherwise, as a practical matter, the promise for his full denial breakthrough may be downgraded. Accordingly, the counselor could choose "to fight fire with fire," asking Mike if he has experienced feelings of desperation and hopelessness, and if he has ever contemplated suicide, defined a suicide plan, or intended to implement the plan. Although this portion of the dialogue may be painful for Mike, these questions are clinically essential in view of evidence suggesting that intense gambling cravings occur during periods of suicidal ideation, and that suicidality is high among pathological gamblers (Petry & Kiluk, 2002). Further reports from Gamblers Anonymous indicate approximately 66% of all pathological gamblers have contemplated suicide; 47% were able to describe a definite suicide plan; and 77% stated that they would prefer death over a gambling life (National Gambling Impact Study Commission, 1999).

The Role of Family

Over the last two decades, gambling activities have increased dramatically, and an alarming number of children are growing up in households in which pathological gambling is a problem. Research exists demonstrating children model gambling behaviors, whereby the children of pathological gamblers are significantly more likely to develop negative gambling behaviors than are children whose parents or caregivers are nonpathological gamblers. More unfortunate are markers that inform powerful intrafamily relationships between substance abuse, violence, and pathological gambling (Vander-Bilt & Franklin, 2003).

The counselor states that Mike regrets the strained relationships he has with his children and has committed to drawing closer to his children. Thus, it is assumed that the counselor and Mike have engaged in at least preliminary discussions concerning Mike's family life. Returning to the notions of gambling and suicide among pathological gamblers, and considering issues of social learning, substance abuse, and violence occurring within gambling families, the counselor could probe more deeply into Mike's family's environment. As a safety matter, the counselor can begin these conversations by assessing (reassessing) Mike's family for substance abuse, violence, and firearms accessibility. Moving forward, the counselor could ask Mike to describe his daughter's and son's thoughts and feelings about Mike's gambling. Mike could be further prodded about whether he has any evidence suggesting his daughter or son has experimented with gambling, and more specifically, Internet gambling.

Ideally, the counselor would merge these conversations with pertinent information regarding the apparent ease with which youngsters and adolescents can access Internet gambling opportunities. The counselor can describe disturbing statistics referencing current numbers of adolescent pathological gamblers and ponder aloud the overall upsetting realities of suicidality among pathological gamblers. Moreover, the counselor should bring to Mike's awareness that according to national statistics, suicide remains the third leading cause of death among young people ages 15 to 24 years, and that the gross proportion (86%) of dying adolescents are male (Anderson & Smith, 2003). Altogether, these data are compelling; and after discussing them with Mike, the counselor could ask his client to contemplate once again any unacceptable costs corresponding to the heady benefits associated with gambling (i.e., power, freedom, and fun). In other words, Mike needs to understand that his decision to gamble certainly carries negative consequences for him, including threats of depression, hopelessness, suicidal ideation, and worse. However, Mike's decision to gamble may carry equally dire consequences for his children. Mike must wonder to himself whether or not he can live with these consequences.

In addition to the addiction's negative impact on his children, Mike's marriage has apparently suffered as well. A survey conducted by the National Opinion Research Center (1999) indicates that approximately 54% of pathological gamblers experience divorce sometime in their lives. Mike's propensity for blaming Audrey, together with his belief that she is his "trigger" and has always been "on his back," may be indicative of profound couple difficulties. On the other hand, addiction specialists understand that whereas all counseling issues (e.g., marital) deserve clinical attention, no additional issues can be reasonably addressed as long as some form of addiction is on board. The fact that Mike continues to express the belief that there is something about Audrey, or about his relationship with Audrey, which "causes" him to gamble corroborates the notion that, for now, the primary counseling issue is Mike's gambling addiction. Clinically speaking, once the gambling addiction issue is attended, additional counseling concerns (e.g., marital) may be assessed and treated, provided the client desires treatment.

Returning to the notion of cost-benefit analysis, the counselor could explore with Mike the ways in which gambling has cost his marriage. For example, the counselor should ask Mike to name the person who has been historically responsible for meeting monthly living expenses. Given Mike's current employment status, combined with his gambling, work, and legal history, it seems likely that he has been challenged to contribute consistently to the family's basic financial survival. Mike must understand that financial instability strikes at the core of any family's sense of security, and that it is logical to assume Audrey and his children view his behaviors as unreliable, perhaps even threatening.

Mike may question whether he is still in love with Audrey; thus, inviting Mike to think out loud about the general value of intimate relationships could be helpful. The counselor may want to pose a question about Mike's current level of desire for a loving and intimate connection. The counselor also could ask Mike to describe a time when he felt love and desire for Audrey. Moving on, the counselor should introduce discussions about Audrey's current familial status. Does she generate any loving feelings at all? How does Mike view her relationship with the children? Is she a loving and caring mother? Does she nurture the children? Do they love and nurture her? Who is loving and nurturing Mike?

As an activity, gambling alone probably produces and sustains feelings of personal power; yet, Mike needs to understand that his ability to partake of these "power flights" may be necessarily limited to and supported by Audrey. Accordingly, one possible discussion thread could surround routine family life (e.g., "When you're out gambling, who's making dinner?"). The counselor should then reverse the question, asking Mike if he remembers occasions in the past when he enjoyed dinner with his family, and if he ever misses the intimacy of the family dinner table. Freedom is by definition partially reflected in the notion of escape. The counselor might ask Mike to ponder times spent gambling, while "escaping from" Audrey, children, home, responsibility, work, and worry. If Mike counters indicating that when in gambling throes he rarely if ever thinks about Audrey and the kids, then the counselor should encourage Mike to wonder about any precipitating factors surrounding the desire to escape. In other words, clinically speaking, it would be helpful to ascertain whether or not Audrey is "the trigger," or if Mike's desire to escape from her and all she represents—adult responsibility—is the actual "trigger." Accordingly, Mike should be queried about whether or not he presently longs to "escape from" Audrey and other worries, or if memories of past "escapes" currently conjure pleasurable feelings, including ones of empowerment and liberation. Finally, the counselor will want to talk with Mike about fun and lighthearted elements of his marriage. The fact that Mike describes his wife as always "on his back" suggests that his marital relationship has decompensated to the point at which there are no notable fun times. If so, then from Mike's point of view, this labor-intensive domestic backdrop may provide an emotionally and psychologically necessary foil to, and excuse for, his need to have fun. The counselor should consider helping Mike draw a connection between any anxious internal feelings that bring on desires for escape and freedom and his behavioral decision to permit himself to "have some fun"—or to gamble.

Alternative Treatments and Counselor Responsibility

As was previously mentioned, career counseling may be a useful option for Mike. In other words, Mike's discovery of new or amended career possibilities could provide him with a view of how life after addiction may be different, improved, and exciting. Much evidence exists suggesting that addictions are a systemic problem and must be treated accordingly. Thus, the counselor could recommend family counseling. Finally, although the counselor must recognize and maintain appropriate professional limitations, he or she may want to encourage Mike to engage in spiritual-based conversations. It is unclear whether or not Mike lives with a faith system, even though it may be assumed that spiritual discussions occur with Gamblers Anonymous. Nonetheless, at 46 years old, Mike is developmentally poised to explore his life's meaning and purpose, and to wonder how he cares to live the time he has left.

In closing, the counselor ponders follow-up with Mike. In the strictest sense, the counselor has no direct responsibility unless he or she suspects suicidality, homicidality, child endangerment, or psychosis. It may be assumed that these issues were reasonably addressed in counseling. Beyond that, the counselor could have considered coconstructing a plan with Mike regarding a follow-up bolstering phone call or letter, asking Mike if a phone call or letter, placed at a specific interval past the last session, would be acceptable. Yet, it is important to remember that ultimately Mike is in charge of his counseling experience—and his recovery.

■References

American Psychiatric Association. (2000). *Diagnostic and statistical manual of mental disorders* (4th ed., Text Revision). Washington, DC: Author.

Anderson, R. N., & Smith, B. L. (2003). Deaths: Leading causes for 2001. *National Vital Statistics Report 2003, 52,* 1–86.

Associated Press. (2004). *States are addicted to gambling.* Retrieved July 10, 2004, from http://www.gambletribune.org/article921.html

Ferster, C. B. (1958). Intermittent reinforcement of a complex response in a chimpanzee. *Journal of the Experimental Analysis of Behavior, 1,* 163–165.

Gehring, V. (1999). *The American state lottery: Sale or swindle?* College Park: University of Maryland, Institute for Philosophy and Public Policy. Retrieved July 11, 2004, from http://www.puaf.umd.edu/IPPP/Winter-Spring00/The_American_State_Lottery.htm

Glasser, W. (1997). Control theory. In N. Glasser (Ed.), *Control theory in the practice of reality therapy: Case studies* (pp. 1–15). New York: Harper & Row.

Hodgins, D. C., & Makarchuk, K. (2003). Trusting problem gamblers: Reliability and validity of self-reported gambling behavior. *Psychology of Addictive Behaviors, 17,* 244–248.

National Gambling Impact Study Commission. (1999). *Report to the President, Congress, state governors, and tribal leaders.* Washington, DC: Author. Retrieved July 10, 2004, from http://govinfo.library.unt.edu/ngisc/reports/exsum_1-7.pdf

National Opinion Research Center. (1999). *Recent U.S. estimates of the costs of problem gambling.* Chicago: Author. Retrieved July 11, 2004, from http://www.pc.gov.au/inquiry/gambling/finalreport/appendixk.pdf

Petry, N. M., & Kiluk, B. D. (2002). Suicidal ideation and suicide attempts in treatment-seeking pathological gamblers. *Journal of Nervous and Mental Diseases, 190,* 462–469.

Potenza, M. N., Steinberg, M. A., Skudlarski, P., Fulbright, R. K., Lacadie, C. M., Wilber, M. K., et al. (2003). Gambling urges in pathological gambling: A functional magnetic resonance imaging study. *Archives of General Psychiatry, 60,* 828–836.

Vander-Bilt, J., & Franklin, J. (2003). Gambling in a familial context. In H. J. Shaffer & M. N. Hall (Eds.), *Futures at stake: Youth, gambling, and society* (pp. 100–125). Reno: University of Nevada Press.

18 Employee Assistant Programming and Addictions

■Critical Incident

Matthew Kent Mayberry

Background

Tommy is an 18-year-old White male who has been employed as a janitor for a large company for 6 months. He was referred to the Employee Assistance Program (EAP) following an incident with his supervisor. Tommy had come into work late this particular morning smelling of alcohol and acting belligerently toward his supervisor and coworkers. This was the latest in a series of similar, well-documented episodes. He was given the choice of agreeing to be evaluated for substance abuse and attending counseling, if deemed appropriate, or being released from his job.

Tommy grew up in the projects, being raised by his mother in a single-parent household. His mother, 56, does not work. His father was never married to his mother and moved out of the house before Tommy started school. His father is now married to another woman and has moved to another city. Tommy still lives at home with his mother and two younger brothers. He admitted to drinking a case of beer every day and smoking three to four marijuana joints on the weekends. He said that his mother smoked marijuana while he was growing up and had told him that it was not a drug. This is a fairly well-entrenched idea for him.

He said that he did not feel safe growing up in the projects and still does not. Tommy is smaller in stature, and there are big boys who like to pick fights with him. They all jump on him if he wins. He said that there are drugs in the neighborhood, but he does not sell.

Tommy dropped out of school in 10th grade after having numerous altercations with his teachers and having been arrested four times for drinking-related incidents that occurred away from school. He said that he stopped going to school because the teachers said he was doing stuff that he didn't do. He had been suspended from school several times, for such incidents as fighting, talking back, skipping school, and being tardy.

During his academic career, he had been retained in a grade three times. He said that his teachers did not like him because he has been held back so many times. Tommy had been having problems since the first grade. He was retained in first, second, and third grades. Finally, out of frustration, one day he walked out of the classroom and never went back. He was able to later pass the GED.

He has several friends whom he gets into trouble with while drinking. He has stolen a car. He also took part in a drive-by shooting. He was shot at and so he and his friends shot at the boys. He does not know if anybody was hurt. He said that he would do it again if someone were to threaten him. His friends wanted him to take part in a robbery, but he did not want to.

He has attempted suicide two different times within the past 2 years. The first time, he used a knife. The second time, he tried to jump out of a window. He decided to try suicide because he did not get enough attention. He said that others in the neighborhood pick on him because he is short. That makes him mad. He was not thinking about suicide at the time of the interview.

He has been arrested four times for incidents that occurred while he has been drinking. The first time was for attacking his aunt. They had had a disagreement when his aunt had come to visit his family. He said that his aunt slapped him and he slapped her back. On three other occasions, Tommy was arrested for underage drinking.

Since starting to work for his new employer, Tommy has had several problems related to his drinking. He is often late for work because he is hung over from partying the night before, and his attitude has been poor. He reported that he often argued back and forth with supervisors and fellow employees. He said that they would get mad when he got the best of them. Tommy denies that this situation is his fault and said that similar things have happened with all his employers. He said that he felt as if the employers were being unfair because they tolerate the same behaviors from other employees. This makes him mad. He said that while others do not get into trouble, he gets reprimanded. He said that he wants to keep his job because he needs money to buy more alcohol.

Incident

Tommy referred himself to the EAP because of deteriorating work performance and difficulty with interpersonal relationships, both due to his drinking-related behavior. A comprehensive evaluation was conducted, including the Alcohol Use Disorders Identification Test, Drug Abuse Screening Test, and the Outlook Questionnaire 45. Because of suspected alcohol dependence, Tommy was referred to a psychiatrist for additional evaluation.

During our initial interview, Tommy presented as anxious and somewhat reluctant to discuss the events that led to his being referred to the employee substance abuse program. He was in denial that he had done anything wrong. He said that he thought it was unfair to be asked to refer himself to the EAP because he was in control of his drinking and the arguments with his supervisor and coworkers were not his fault. He said that he needed money to buy more alcohol, so he was willing to get help.

Tommy was admitted to the 6-week outpatient substance abuse program. It was explained to him that there are two minimum requirements for participation: First, he must abstain from all use of alcohol and illicit drugs while enrolled; and second, he must attend a group counseling session once a week. He was also encouraged to attend Alcoholics Anonymous. The psychiatrist recommended to Tommy that he use Antabuse (disulfiram), which he reported doing.

During the 6 weeks, Tommy completed various written and reading assignments. These included writing an autobiography, which helped him identify the risk factors in his family background, upbringing, and current lifestyle; reading from 12-step literature; and preparing a survival plan and daily journal. During weekly therapy sessions, Tommy was able to process and examine his problems in depth. The group members and I were able to facilitate open communication and to help Tommy with his self-discovery.

Discussion

Tommy began the long journey of realizing and accepting his alcohol-related problems. He said that before he began counseling, he did not know that he had a greater likelihood than many people to abuse alcohol because of his genetics and the attitudes toward drugs and alcohol he encountered in his home and neighborhood while growing up. He also said he learned that while he thought the drinking was helping him deal with the stress in his life, it was actually having the opposite effect. The drinking had taken control over him and was causing stress. Having gained this insight, he reported that he intends to not use in the future and plans to continue to attend AA meetings.

Questions

1. Should employees be required to submit to substance abuse treatment as a condition of further employment?
2. What techniques might have been used to work with the employee on an individual basis?
3. How should comorbid problems (i.e., depression) be dealt with? While the EAP offers limited outpatient substance abuse treatment, the company does not offer other mental health services.

■Response

Ford Brooks

Question 1

The first question asks whether employees should be required to submit to substance abuse treatment as a condition of further employment. Many companies, at the onset of employment, have informed policies regarding alcohol and drug use and the consequences or treatment referrals should they become needed. Companies typically will require prospective employees to submit a urine sample for drug screening. Should they become employed, random urine screens throughout their employment could be requested. The combination of positive urine screens for drugs, a pattern of missed days, and intoxication on the job would typically indicate the need for a substance abuse evaluation or treatment.

This particular incident presents Tommy as intoxicated on the job as well as having other occasions in which he had been late as a result of hangovers. In addition to being informed about the policies, Tommy should be informed that his safety, as well as the safety of others, is paramount where his intoxication potentially put others at risk. Therefore, the requirement for substance abuse treatment is very appropriate in Tommy's case, and he should submit to a substance abuse treatment program. In some instances, however, companies will automatically terminate employment and provide no second chances. In this company he is fortunate to be given an opportunity to examine his drinking.

Question 2

Regarding the question of what techniques might have been used to work with the employee on an individual basis, prior to Tommy's intoxication on the job site, he could have been referred for individual counseling pertaining to anger management issues and difficulty in getting along with peers. In the incident description, it is clear how Tommy seeks attention through his behavior. An initial referral before this incident (anger management issues) may have been helpful in allowing Tommy a therapeutic environment to begin the exploration of his feelings and begin connecting how his drinking and anger affect his life. The use of motivational interviewing techniques in an individual counseling modality along with participation in group treatment and AA meetings could be an appropriate recommendation. Tommy's life reportedly has been difficult and absent of individual attention other than through attention raised by his negative behavior. An individual counselor, preferably male because of the absence of his father, might prove to enhance what has already been recommended and help Tommy develop a trusting relationship with a male figure. I would suggest that Tommy engage in individual counseling as an additional aspect to his treatment but not as the only aspect to his treatment plan.

Question 3

Question 3 asks how comorbid problems should be dealt with. While the EAP offers limited outpatient substance abuse treatment, the company does not offer other mental health services.

From what has been presented in this case, alcohol dependence, major recurrent depression, and a possible learning disability are the headlining clinical issues. It appears a psychiatrist has been involved; however, it was not clear for what purpose (a medication evaluation for depression or an additional addic-

Critical Incidents in Addictions Counseling

tion evaluation). Based on the question, the EAP counselor will need to be familiar with the community-based options for treatment referral (learning disabilities, mental health counseling, and medication management/monitoring). Even though Tommy may have insurance, he will also need a referral into the community mental health system to provide him with a full array of appropriate services. This means the EAP counselor will need to be the coordinator and facilitator for both the substance abuse services and the mental health services being provided in the community.

This particular client has the potential to fall through the cracks of the mental health substance abuse system. The EAP counselor in this case will act as a bridge between substance abuse and mental health services. The counselor's role will be to facilitate appropriate referrals to the mental health system, and at the same time provide communication with substance abuse treatment.